Elements
of
Interviewing

The Elements of Interviewing

Kenneth G. Shipley

California State University, Fresno

Julie McNulty Wood

Fresno, California

Singular Publishing Group, Inc.

San Diego · London

Singular Publishing Group, Inc.
4284 41st Street
San Diego, California 92105-1197

19 Compton Terrace
London, N1 2UN, UK

© 1996 by Singular Publishing Group, Inc.

Typeset in 10/12 Bookman by So Cal Graphics
Printed in the United States of America by McNaughton & Gunn

Library of Congress Cataloging-in-Publication Data

Shipley, Kenneth G.
   The elements of interviewing / Kenneth G. Shipley, Julie McNulty
   Wood.
      p.   cm.
   Includes bibliographical references and index.
   ISBN 1-56593-601-9
   1. Interviewing.   2. Intercultural communication.   I. Wood, Julie
McNulty.   II. Title.
BF637 . I5S45 1995
158'.39—dc20   95-34231
                                                        CIP

Contents

Preface

Virtually everyone beyond early childhood has interviewed others and been interviewed. Interviews occur on a daily basis within our occupations or professions, in choosing certain products or services, in selling a product or service, as part of teaching or being a student, in managing a household, and countless other activities. Many people engage in interviews frequently, but surprisingly few of us have specific training or education on the basics of interviewing. A common complaint of many people, working in a variety of fields, is that their real training in interviewing ends up coming by trial and error. This is certainly a difficult way to learn. It is also an inefficient and sometimes ineffective way to learn—just because we gain experience by trial and error does not necessarily mean we discover some of the basic principles of effective interviewing.

The purpose of this book is to outline the most important elements of interviewing in a concise, practical, and easy-to-read manner. To do this, we adapted the format for this book from two outstanding works: Strunk and White's (1979) *The Elements of Style* and Meier and Davis' (1993) *The Elements of Interviewing*. Strunk and White's *The Elements of Style* is a classic resource of English grammar usage. This little book is one of the most readable, concise, and popular books on the basics of English grammar ever written. Borrowing on Strunk and White's format, Scott Meier wrote *The Elements of Counseling* in 1989. Meier outlined the fundamentals of counseling in a concise, to-the-point fashion within his book. *The Elements of Counseling* has been very popular with students, professionals, and others interested in the area of counseling. A second edition of this book, coauthored by Susan Davis, was published in 1993.

We had used *The Elements of Style* for a long time, but it was after reading *The Elements of Counseling* that the idea occurred to address the area of interviewing within such a format. Thus, borrowing on the formats used by these resources, our goal is to present the basic elements of interviewing in a concise, readable, practical manner. We have tried to take the most important principles of interviewing—irrespective of whether the reader is a student, professional, or other interested party and irrespective of anyone's particular occupation or profession. In effect, we have tried to identify and present those items common to effective interviewing in a variety of situations or settings.

The book is organized under 88 headings, or topic areas, which are found within the seven chapters. References cited throughout the book are located at the end of the book. A subject and an author index are also found at the end of the book.

The primary focus of the book is an outline of the basic tenets of interviewing that cross settings and disciplines and are applicable to most interview situations. However, there are some important cross-cultural variables that can affect interviews. We have tried to identify some of these differences within the text. However, there is a danger in identifying differences if it leads to overgeneralizing or stereotyping individuals from any cultural background. Our purpose is not to "typify" members of any group; rather, it is to describe certain variables and factors that may influence certain interviews with some individuals from linguistically or culturally diverse backgrounds.

We thank a number of people who were immensely helpful during the development and production of this book. Celeste Roseberry-McKibbin, in particular, was extremely helpful with her insights, comments, and suggestions. The staff and consultants at Singular Publishing Group, particularly Marie Linvill, Pam Rider, Angie Singh, Sadanand Singh, and Randy Stevens, provided excellent assistance and guidance during the review and production process. Our respective families provided us the opportunities to undertake this project and were encouraging and helpful throughout the undertaking. Special appreciation and our love is extended to Peggy and Jennifer Shipley, Ryan Wood, and John and Margie McNulty.

We hope you enjoy the book and benefit from it. Please feel free to contact the publisher with specific comments or suggestions.

CHAPTER
1

Fundamental Characteristics of Interviews

Interviews are conducted every day in various places: at work, in offices, in homes, on the street, by telephone, at sporting events—even in cars and on various forms of public transportation. Interviews occur in a wide variety of fields, occupations, and professions. Interviewing someone else or being interviewed are common and important activities. However, if asked to define interviewing, many of us would be hard pressed to define the term beyond it being a conversation involving the asking or answering of questions. There are, however, several basic elements of interviewing, as well as specific factors that help ensure success in interviewing. Let's begin by looking at some of the basic factors involved in interviews.

1. *An interview is a serious conversation with a specific purpose.*

Interviewing involves **a serious conversation that is conducted for a specific purpose** (Stewart & Cash, 1994). We tend to think of interviewing as being a somewhat formal type of exchange in which one person asks questions and someone else responds to the questions asked. We also tend to think of interviewing as something that occurs on television talk shows, during employment interviews, with job performance reviews, by reporters collecting news, and so forth. However, interviews are essentially serious conversations that involve specific purposes. In this way, interviewing occurs every day in a wide variety of situations in which two or more people get together for specific purposes. Let's compare a general conversation with an interview.

General conversations can be observed almost anywhere. They occur at work, at school, in the home, at the market, on the street, and so forth. Most of us engage in some form of conversation each day. One basic type of conversation we engage in involves exchanging social pleasantries. The teller at a bank asks, "How are you today?" and the customer responds, "Fine, thank-you." Perhaps the two parties then engage in a few moments of casual discussion about the weather or some other light-hearted topic. As interviewing has been defined here, we would not consider this to be an interview situation because there is no serious purpose to the conversation other than engaging in a socially appropriate exchange.

A different form of conversation occurs with a more specific purpose in mind. A counselor or a physician, for example, asks a patient, "How are you doing today?" The patient, likely realizing the serious purpose of the question, probably provides a rather detailed description of any difficulties being experienced. When a conversation is steered by a specific purpose, it may very well be an interview.

A serious conversation with a specific purpose is seen in many human activities, including employment interviews, during job performance reviews, and by college students picking which school to attend, pollsters trying to identify the public's perceptions and feelings, detectives trying to solve a crime, insurance agents determining their clients' needs, physicians attempting to determine a diagnosis, telemarketers trying to sell their products, salespeople in furniture stores, and many more. These examples illustrate just a few of the types of conversations conducted for a specific purpose and, therefore, involving this basic element of interviewing.

2. Interviews need a purpose and a plan of action, plus a good communication exchange.

A fundamental element of an interview is having a serious purpose. Two other basic elements are having a plan of action for the interview and for communication to occur between the parties involved (Dillard & Reilly, 1988). Fenlason (1962) suggested that having a **predetermined purpose** distinguishes interviews from other types of conversations. The predetermined purpose serves as a guide for the course of the exchange. Otherwise, the interaction is probably more of a social conversation or perhaps a poor, aimless, or meandering interview. Interviews without a specific purpose are often weak, ineffective, and sometimes very frustrating to either or both parties involved.

The second fundamental aspect of interviewing is having a **plan of action**. Without some form of plan, there is little direction to the interaction. Effective interviewers enter an interview situation with some plan in mind about what needs to be addressed and how they will proceed. Of course, what they cover and how they actually proceed can change once they are involved in the interview, but interviewers need an initial "game plan" going into the interview.

The third aspect of an interview is having **good communication** between both parties. Certainly there is little to be gained from any interview in which effective communication does not happen. Optimal communication tends to occur in the presence of having a predetermined purpose, a plan of action, basic technical skills in interviewing, and several basic personality qualities appropriate to engendering good communication. Some of the basic personality qualities necessary for effective interviewing are discussed in Chapter 2 and some of the important technical skills for interviewing are described in Chapters 3–6.

3. *Interviews typically consist of two parties and address both objective and subjective types of information.*

Interviews usually involve **two parties**, irrespective of the number of people involved. These two parties include one who is interviewing and the other who is being interviewed. For example, one interviewer could interview an entire family. In this case, the interviewer is one party and the family being interviewed is the other. An example with even more people, but still involving only two parties, would be one company's board of directors interviewing a second company's board of directors to help determine whether or not to buy the company. There are still only two parties to this interaction—those interviewing and those being interviewed.

The roles of the two parties can shift during an interview. One party may start out as the interviewer but end up being interviewed. For example, a physician interviews a patient to identify some illness; but, in the course of the discussion, the patient essentially assumes the role of interviewer to determine whether or not he is "sold" on the physician and her recommendations. Realize that this can happen in some interviews; it may be very appropriate in some circumstances (for example, also interviewing the physician), but it may be inappropriate to the interviewer's purposes in other circumstances. Interviews can include both objective and subjective types of information. Interviewing provides interviewers with opportunities to ask objective as well as subjective types of questions, or to discuss both objectively and subjectively based information. **Objective** information includes verifiable information, such as someone's age, sex, grade, specific dates, something that happened or did not happen, and so forth. The interviewer may need to learn about objectively based information, such as basic facts, dates, or events important to the purpose of the interview. The interviewer may also inquire about **subjective** information, which includes interviewees' impressions or interpretations of certain facts, or their attitudes or feelings about certain subjects. For example, someone might relate that they are 16 years of age, which is objective information. That person might also relate that being 16 is frustrating for various reasons, which is more subjective information.

Subjective information often provides valuable insights that cannot be obtained from basic facts alone. For example, a school-age child isn't wearing her glasses. This basic, verifiable fact can be observed. Discussion with the child or parent may reveal that the youngster is embarrassed about wearing glasses and, therefore, is refusing to wear them. This is subjectively based, but potentially important information. Thus, both objectively and subjectively based information can be valuable.

4. *Interviews typically involve getting information, giving information, or influencing, persuading, or counseling.*

So far, we have touched on several fundamental principles of interviewing. Now let's turn our attention to the basic types of interviews. Stewart and Cash (1994), two of America's foremost authorities on interviewing, outline the different types of interviews as follows:

A. Information giving
1. Orientation
2. Training, instruction, coaching
3. Job-related instructions

B. Information gathering
1. Surveys and polls
2. Exit interviews
3. Research interviews

    4. Investigations: insurance, police, etc.
    5. Medical, psychological, case history, diagnostic, case-worker, etc.
    6. Journalistic

C. Selection
    1. Screening
    2. Determinate [i.e., determining something]
    3. Placement

D. Problems of interviewee's behavior
    1. Appraisal, evaluative, review
    2. Separation, firing
    3. Correction, discipline, reprimand
    4. Counseling

E. Problems of interviewer's behavior
    1. Receiving complaints
    2. Grievances
    3. Receiving suggestions

F. Problem solving
    1. Discussing mutually shared problems
    2. Receiving suggestions for solutions

G. Persuasion
    1. Selling products and services
    2. Recruiting members
    3. Fundraising and development
    4. Changing the way a party feels, thinks, or acts (p. 6)

This is an excellent list of the various types and functions of interviews. However, for our purposes here, we are going to simplify this 25-item list by looking at all interviewing as having one of three major functions. Specifically:

- To learn more about someone or something, in effect, to gather or get information.
- To provide or give information.
- To counsel, persuade, or to influence or alter the feelings, attitudes, or actions of another party.

As you look through Stewart and Cash's (1994) list, notice how each of these different interview functions essentially falls into one of these three basic functions (to get information, to give information, or to influence, persuade, or counsel). Now let's give each of these types of interviews a name. First, interviews in which we attempt to gather information or to learn more about something or someone can be called **information-getting interviews**. Second, when we give or provide information, we conduct **information-giving interviews**. And third, when we attempt to alter or influence someone else's attitudes, feelings, or behavior, we conduct **influencing, persuasive, or counseling interviews.** Several examples of these interview types should help illustrate these basic interview functions:

Examples of information-getting interviews.

- When a nurse or physician interviews a patient to determine where pain is felt or if a problem has been resolved.
- When a bank officer talks to a loan applicant to determine the need for and use of a potential loan.
- When a police officer talks with witnesses to determine what may have happened at a crime scene.
- When a school administrator interviews several candidates for a teaching position.
- When a journalist talks to a group of politicians about how they intend to vote on a particular issue.
- When a homeowner talks to several contractors before deciding who will build a room addition.

Note that in each example the interviewer is trying to obtain certain types of information, hence the name **information-getting interviews.**

Examples of information-giving interviews:

- When a physician sits down with a patient to explain a diagnosis and suggested course of treatment.
- When a bank officer sits down with loan applicants and shares that, although the entire amount requested cannot be lent, a smaller loan can be approved.
- When a teacher meets with parents to explain how a child is doing in class and shares some observations about the child.
- When an employer sits down with a job applicant, offers the job, and describes the basic job expectations and duties.
- When an insurance agent describes basic insurance packages available.

The interviewer is providing information in each of these examples; therefore, we call them **information-giving interviews**. The basic purpose of information-giving interviews is to provide information rather than trying to persuade, counsel, or in some way influence or change someone else's feelings or actions.

When we try to influence someone else to feel differently or to act in some way, we use an **influencing, persuasive,** or **counseling interview**. Unlike the information-giving interview in which we just provide information, counseling-type interviews attempt to promote some type of change within the other party. The desired change may be how someone feels about a subject or about another person or it may be to produce some other specific type of action.

Examples of influencing, persuasive, or counseling interviews:
- When the physician has discussed several treatment options, but attempts to influence which option believed to be best to pursue.
- When a bank officer attempts to talk a loan applicant into revising plans to fit within the amount of money that can be loaned.
- When a teacher attempts to engage a caregiver in specific activities to implement at home to remedy difficulties being seen in the classroom.
- When an employer attempts to counsel an employee to be on time or to get along better with co-workers.
- When an insurance company representative makes a specific proposal believed to be the best package for the client and attempts to "sell" the package.
- When someone tries to persuade a friend to stop engaging in some form of self-destructive behavior or other undesirable activity.

Again, look at most interviews and you will find one of three functions: getting information; giving information; or attempts to influence, persuade, or counsel. Realize also that a given interview can include more than one of these functions, such as both giving information and trying to persuade about some specific action.

5. *There can be apprehension in either party.*

Apprehension is common in many interviews. It is important to realize that apprehension, perhaps even some degree of fear, occurs within a number of interview situations. The very nature of interviews, with both the interviewer and the party being interviewed being "on the spot," is a source of apprehension. For the interviewer, wanting to make a good impression can be a source of concern or fear. There can also be fears of not knowing precisely what to ask—or fear of being asked some question that cannot be answered. The interviewer may be concerned that the other party will not cooperate fully. In some settings, interviewers may be uncertain if their advice or counsel is being understood or accepted. Interviews conducted across cultures can cause apprehension, particularly if either party is uncomfortable with members of another culture. There are, of course, other possible sources of uncertainty, fear, or discomfort.

Those being interviewed also have many possible sources of fear or concern. A list of potential fears could be very large, depending on the type of interview. Just a few examples include:

- Will the interviewer like me?
- Will the interviewer be nice or be understanding?
- Will the interviewer be able to help?
- Is the interviewer going to try to trick me, to try to convince me to do something, or to try to sell me something?
- Will I have the information or know the facts that I may be asked about?
- Will the interviewer believe me?
- Will I say something that I shouldn't and regret it later?

Again, this is just a brief listing of possible apprehensions an interviewee may have. Such factors or concerns, which often go unsaid, produce a certain level of tension or concern, particularly in new situations.

Such apprehensions may be felt by the interviewer, the party being interviewed, or even both parties. For those who are doing the interviewing, such tensions or apprehensions usually diminish across time and experience. For all interviewers—beginning or experienced—some of our natural apprehensions can be reduced by knowing our field well and by having a specific purpose and a specific plan of action in mind when entering into an interview situation. It is also helpful to simply recognize that apprehensions exist and are very normal. The various techniques and principles of interviewing in the chapters that follow will help interviewers conduct appropriate interviews. This can help reduce some of the apprehension and fears that an interviewer can take into any interaction.

6. *Digressions often occur in interviews.*

The term **digression** here means to wander from the main purpose or subject being discussed, rather than in the more psychological sense such as moving back into the past to explore unresolved issues or underlying meanings. Digressions that wander from the main purpose or subject of discussion are natural occurrences in many interviewing situations. Most conversations of any type do not move in a straight line from point A to point Z. Rather, some subject is discussed and, perhaps before either party realizes it, another topic is being discussed. If the first topic was unfinished, the participants probably move back to the original topic at some point. The same thing occurs within interviews. The participants may begin discussing some subject, then skip to another subject, and later return to the unfinished topic. It is important to realize that, as interviews are a form of human conversation, digressions are an inherent aspect of interviews that should not be feared or always discourage inexperienced interviewers.

Digressions need to be recognized and, depending on their frequency and nature, they often need to be controlled by the interviewer. Too many digressions, too much time spent within digressions, or digressions that lead conversations into inappropriate areas of discussion can be counterproductive to the purposes of an interview. The first step in controlling digressions is realizing that digressions occur for different reasons. One reason is simply that the interviewee has forgotten the topic of discussion. In this event, prompting or cueing the interviewee about the topic being addressed can help refocus the conversation. Another type of digression is when someone returns to some topic they do not yet feel has been fully explained or has not been understood or agreed upon. It is also possible that the parties simply begin talking about an area that leads into another area. Before they know it, the parties are discussing subjects that are completely unrelated to the goals at hand. Note that each of these different factors could be a reason for digression.

Another type of digression seen in some interviews is the "recurrent theme" (Shipley, 1992). A recurrent theme is some particular question or concern that keeps reemerging throughout an interview. For example, an interviewee asks about the costs of a product several times, a job applicant persists in asking about certain aspects of the job, a student sent to the principal's office asks several times if his parents are going to be contacted, and so forth. In each of these cases, by returning to the recurrent theme, the interviewee shows concern about some particular subject (cost of the product, job benefits, or if the parents will be contacted in these examples). The recurrent theme subject reoccurs because it is of real concern.

Knowing how to handle a digression requires that we first recognize its presence. This allows the interviewer to respond appropriately. For example, the interviewer may need to exercise greater self-discipline to avoid entering into general, nonpurpose-related digressions; may need to address a concern that keeps reoccurring; or some other alternative. However, until a digression is recognized, there is no basis for doing anything to redirect the interview.

7. Conduct an interview only when necessary.

Interviews are conducted when information cannot be collected or conveyed adequately or as well in some other way. For example, when applying for a job, the applicant fills out an application from which the employer gains various details about the applicant's history. However, the application may only allow partial insight into the applicant's abilities or attitudes about work or the job, or how well the person might fit into the work situation. Thus, an interview is often conducted to verify information about the application, get a sense of the individual's experience and abilities, gain insight into the person's work characteristics and how the applicant gets along with others, and so forth. This type of information and insight may not be possible by simply reviewing a written application form.

Similarly, an insurance agent or financial planner needs to explore a client's needs, aspirations, and goals before making specific recommendations. A child psychologist or special education teacher would be very remiss by just mailing a diagnosis to a concerned parent rather than communicating in person with the other party. And a sales counselor would be hard-pressed to make many sales without personal contact. Each of these are examples in which some form of an interview is necessary and appropriate. There are times, however, when information can be gathered or shared without an interview. Application forms, letters, memoranda, or quick phone calls are just a few examples of other means of working with information.

As a general rule, conduct an interview only when information cannot be gained, shared, or behaviors or attitudes changed as effectively and efficiently by other means. Interviews are time consuming, so doing an interview only when needed is an efficient use of our time and the time of others.

8. Every interview has a conductor; it should be the interviewer.

Sales offices have a manager, corporations have a CEO, football teams have a coach, schools have a principal, classes have a teacher, orchestras have a conductor, organizing groups have a spokesperson, and so forth. The same principle applies to most professions—law, education, health care, the sciences, and others. People often see a professional with an expectation that this person will have certain insight or answers, will be "in charge," and will provide direction and focus to the endeavor. For both interviewers and interviewees, it can be very frustrating to be a part of a "leaderless interview." This can be particularly frustrating for interviewees who come from a relatively authoritarian, hierarchal social structure or culture. As described earlier, the interviewer needs to understand the purpose of the interview and have a plan of action in mind. This becomes the basis for providing appropriate direction to the conversations that ensue.

There are usually a couple of major reasons why interviewees "take over" an interview. Several of these include interviewees do not have confidence in the interviewer; they are unsure where an interaction is heading; interviewees disagree with where the interaction is heading; or they are, for some reason, very aggressive, hostile, or controlling. These latter causes—the aggressiveness or over-controlling—are the exception. More commonly, interviewees take control of an interaction when the interviewer is failing to provide appropriate direction. It is as if "no one else is steering the ship, so someone had better." This is usually preventable when the interviewer is competent, confident, knows what needs to be done, and acts with a specific plan in mind.

CHAPTER 2

Characteristics and Factors in Effective Interviewing

Everyone involved in interviewing can learn to conduct more successful, productive interviews. As noted in Chapter 1, the interviewer is the "conductor" of an effective interview. The conductor needs to have a specific purpose, a plan of action, and be able to foster effective communication. There are many personal qualities and skills associated with effective interviewing, including good observational skills; good listening skills; the abilities to develop and maintain rapport; sensitivity and courtesy; an understanding of other people and how to deal effectively with people of different age levels, cultural backgrounds, and the same and opposite gender; and generally being a wise person. These are primary areas discussed in this chapter.

1. *Observe carefully.*

An important technique for obtaining information and insight while interviewing is observation of behavior: frowning, sighing, halting or tentative speech, eye contact aversion, looking away, fidgeting, consistency or inconsistency between what is said and how it is said, nodding in agreement, smiling, or others. Good observational skills increase with practice, backed up by a considerable amount of hard work (Emerick & Haynes, 1986; Shipley, 1992). The skilled observer will have the ability to see, hear, and sense specific details in a person's behavior that a less-sophisticated observer would miss. The skilled observer learns to interpret body language and nonverbal cues that provide valuable information about the other party and that party's reactions to what is occurring in an interview.

Someone's body posture can be an indication of how that person feels about being in the situation or something under discussion in an interview. In the Anglo North American culture, a forward-leaning body tilt and open arms tend to indicate that the person being interviewed is feeling comfortable within the interaction and is a willing participant. Conversely, a backward tilting of the body or crossed arms are possible signs of disinterest, resistance, defiance, or even disdain. This can vary across cultures; for example, in some rural Appalachian communities, a relaxed, backward, "belly first" posture is associated with genuine interest, whereas a forward-leaning posture suggests that the other person is unnerved (Keefe, 1988).

Other nonverbal cues can also provide information about an interviewee's interest in the exchange. Someone who is glancing at their watch, clutching a purse, or glancing toward the door is possibly providing cues that they are tiring, distracted, disagreeing, or anxious to leave. If asked, this person might not admit such feelings, but the skilled observer would certainly at least make a mental note of such nonverbal cues.

There are other necessary observations. For example, observing someone's reactions to information given. Does the person seem to be accepting it, ignoring it, thinking about it, or rejecting it? Does the person appear bothered by something being said, ambivalent, or pleased to hear about it? Careful observation helps us assess the impact of certain issues or information. For example, someone who has recently experienced a major loss may report all is going fine, but tears well up in the eyes while saying this. Or, someone who has experienced loss may not yet be feeling the full impact of the loss. Certainly, everything is not yet "fine" in either of these situations.

2. Be objective.

Being objective means not letting your personal emotions or feelings unduly or inappropriately influence your judgments or decisions. This does not mean that an interviewer should be impersonal, aloof, or unfriendly. Rather, having objectivity means not being unduly or inappropriately biased or affected by personal agendas, biases, or forethoughts. Being objective can serve to bolster our abilities to be sensitive to others, as the effects of personal biases and agendas are minimized.

Effective interviewing requires the use of the seemingly conflicting attributes of empathy and objectivity (Rich, 1968). Both, however, are important and achievable. Interviewers need to understand the difference between subjectivity and objectivity and the need to maintain objectivity to conduct good interviews.

3. Cultivate and use good listening skills.

The ability to communicate well is essential for effective interviewing. We tend to think of a good communicator being a skilled or articulate speaker. Certainly being able to express oneself well is important for good communication, but it fails to account for an equally, if not even more important skill—the ability to listen effectively. For interviewing, if we had to choose between someone who was just a good speaker or someone else who was just a good listener, the good listener is the best choice for an interviewer position! Being a good listener is critical for interviews, irrespective of the type of interview being conducted. As Ivey (1994) has commented, "You can't learn about the client if you are doing the talking!" (p. 24).

Listening effectively requires a good deal of concentration and is truly a skill. Careful listening allows the person who is interviewing to gain valuable insights into how interviewees think and how they perceive and feel about information being discussed (Benjamin, 1981). Careful listening not only helps the interviewer begin to understand the interviewee's goals, desires, values, and basic philosophies, but skillful listening also allows the interviewer to understand the presence and types of defense mechanisms and coping strategies the interviewee might be using.

Years ago, Barbara (1958) commented that effective listening is related to four factors: (1) our ability to concentrate, (2) being an active participant in the interaction, (3) the ability to comprehend what is really being said, and (4) being objective. Each of these factors is described briefly. **Concentration** is the ability to focus on the tasks at hand. It requires patience and the abilities to ignore, minimize, or remove any personal or environmental distractions from an interaction. Concentration involves focusing on what is being said and also on any nonverbal behaviors or underlying meanings that occur. Concentration is, above all, being able to focus on all aspects of an interaction at hand without allowing ourself to be distracted from the ongoing process.

Active participation requires that the interviewer's mind be ready, alert, open, flexible, and free from distractions (Shipley, 1992). If the interviewer is thinking about the next appointment, a lunch or dinner appointment, another client, or anything else, the individual is not focusing on the interaction and, therefore, is not fully participating at that time. Active participation helps establish and maintain feelings of rapport and helps ensure that the interviewer is **comprehending** as much as possible at that moment.

Being **objective** was discussed earlier in the chapter. It is important to know the differences between objectivity and subjectivity, and to be capable of listening and reacting without the inappropriate imposition of one's personal attitudes and beliefs on the person being interviewed.

We have already said that effective listening requires a good deal of skill, and most skills are honed through disciplined exercise. Stewart and Cash (1994) describe three basic approaches to or types of listening:

- Listening for comprehension,
- Listening with empathy, and
- Listening for evaluation.

Listening for comprehension usually involves taking in information while providing little or no feedback. The listener tries to absorb and comprehend what the speaker is saying while remaining somewhat detached and objective. The purpose here is to truly understand what the other person is saying and feeling.

Listening with empathy differs from listening for comprehension in that the interviewer becomes somewhat of a reflection of the speaker's emotions. This type of listening allows us to take in the information being conveyed while responding to the speaker in a caring way. The person who is listening with empathy provides warmth, understanding, and reassurance. An understanding of what is being said and how the other party is feeling is demonstrated.

The third type, **listening for evaluation**, involves using the information received to reach some sort of evaluative conclusion. The evaluative listener is listening for information that will explain the speaker's behavior, feelings, actions, condition, or situation. This information may be used to help explain why something was done or felt—or why something was not done or felt.

Listening skills are based, at least in part, on one's own personality, concern for and interest in others, and self-discipline. However, certain situations require different approaches in how one listens. For instance, consider two different scenarios occurring during a bank manager's day. First, the manager is faced with someone who has been mugged on the way home from the bank. The customer's wallet, credit cards, and checkbook were stolen. The manager must get specific information from the victim to properly act in the situation: for example, what should be done first—call the police? call for medical attention? find the victim's family or friends? see if the attacker is still outside? The banker's first task is to **listen for comprehension** to determine how to respond. However, the victim probably also needs an empathetic or sympathetic ear. Thus, once the bank manager understands the situation, the use of **listening with empathy** certainly seems appropriate and useful.

Now let's look at a second example with our bank manager. Another customer, a young adult with a history of an overdrawn checking account and some unpaid bills queries the manager about why a bad credit rating is developing. The manager needs to determine the cause of the customer's problem to help in beginning to straighten out the banking problems. It might be appropriate to spend some time on listening for comprehension and, perhaps, even a little listening with empathy. But, the real focus here will need to be **listening for evaluation**. What is the customer doing or not doing that is creating the problems for the individual and the bank? The banker will probably need to ask some pointed questions to determine what is happening to conduct an overall evaluation of the situation.

From these examples, we can see that an interview may involve more than one type of listening. Depending on what is needed, we should be capable of listening for comprehension, listening with empathy, and listening for evaluation. We should also know when to use the different types of listening and when not to use them. For example, if our customer with the credit problems was simply being irresponsible and was unconcerned that others were not being paid properly, listening with empathy might be very inappropriate. Such listening might even act to encourage undesirable actions. With our mugging victim, listening for evaluation (e.g., carrying too much money, having too many credit cards, walking alone in an unsafe alley behind the building, or whatever) might be appropriate at a later time, but certainly not when initially determining what happened and how to respond.

4. *Don't confuse levels of activity with good listening.*

There is a tendency to assume that, if someone is actively involved in a discussion, they are really listening and constructively participating within the interaction. This is often true, but not always. Kroth (1985) provides an interesting look at this area of activity and listening levels and how they influence communication.

He suggests that there are four different patterns of listening/activity levels within interviews. These are **passive listening, passive nonlistening, active listening**, and **active nonlistening**. These are depicted in Figure 2–1.

Let's look closely at Kroth's model, first recognizing that these are patterns that apply in general to people and their activity/listening levels. Nobody always fits perfectly into only one quadrant; rather, each of us probably has a general tendency to fit within one of the categories. There will be times, however, when we might fit within other categories, depending on what is going on at a given time, our interest in a particular subject, whether we are alert or tired, our levels of concentration, and so forth. Also recognize that this model applies to both parties in an interview—those who interview and those who are interviewed.

Kroth (1985) says that persons in Quadrant A, the **passive listeners**, are nonverbally listening and taking part in the interaction. They may not be very talkative but will exhibit nonverbal signs of

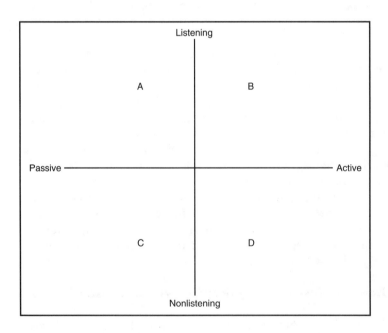

Figure 2–1. A listening paradigm. *Note.* From *Communicating with Parents of Exceptional Children: Improving Parent-Child Relationships* (2nd ed.) (p. 38) by R. L. Kroth, 1985, Denver: Love Publishing Co. Reprinted by permission.

interest, such as smiling with approval or understanding, leaning forward, or nodding their head positively while allowing the speaker the opportunity to talk. People in Quadrant B, the **active listeners**, are both verbally and nonverbally active and they are listening. The active listener is very much a part of the interaction. This type of listener is attentive and shows understanding of the speaker both verbally and nonverbally.

Passive nonlisteners (Quadrant C) are neither listening nor are they active verbally. Sometimes this is very obvious and can be observed in signals of boredom, disinterest, or even of disgust or disdain. There can be little, if any, true communication occurring with someone in Quadrant C. The passive nonlistener may actually be hearing what is going on, but is not listening to the feeling of the message. Kroth (1985) gives the following example of a passive nonlistener:

Wife: I'm so tired, I've been to four stores today trying to find material for a new dress, you're not listening!

Husband: (folding newspaper) You said you've been to four stores looking for material for a new dress.

Although the content was accurate, the husband missed his wife's feeling of fatigue and frustration. (p. 42)

The fourth type of listener in Kroth's model is the **active nonlistener** (Quadrant D). People who are mingling at social gatherings are often active nonlisteners who are "faking interest." The active nonlistener in that situation is the person who goes through the motions of "give and take" and appears to be very much a part of an exchange, but is not really listening to what is being said. At a cocktail party, for example, people may engage and disengage themselves in conversations a number of times. In this type of conversation, these people "talk to" the other party but do not really "talk with" the other party. This can also occur in one-to-one situations such as interviews, with one party talking and appearing to be interested, but not really engaged in much listening or true communication.

Again, no one fits definitively or exclusively into just one of the four categories. People tend to operate as one type of listener most of the time. However, this can change depending on the situation, levels of comfort with the other person, and comfort levels with the topics of conversation. It is also possible for a listener's degree of listening and activity levels to change several times during the same exchange.

It is obvious that certain degrees of listening and activity levels are more conducive to good interviewing than others. Effective interviewers are typically good listeners who are also relatively active within interviews, so Quadrant B is probably a goal for most interviewers. Quadrant A behavior may also be appropriate in some situations, particularly certain information-getting interviews in which the other party is talking freely and openly. Interviewers who tend to be nonlisteners (Quadrants C & D) may be rather ineffective and, although hearing some of what is spoken, may miss potentially important underlying feelings and meanings.

Be aware that there are variations in listening and activity levels within different cultures, so care must be taken when applying Kroth's (1985) model across cultures. Also remember that listening behavior can be influenced by a variety of factors. The physical environment, for example, may cause discomfort and, thereby, hamper good listening and communication. A person who is sitting in an uncomfortable chair, looking into a bright light, or competing with background noise may have considerable difficulties listening effectively. As discussed in Chapter 3, the environment needs to be conducive to appropriate communication.

5. *Develop and maintain rapport.*

The responsibility for the success of any interview or a series of interviews typically lies with the interviewer. One key to success is the development and maintenance of rapport between the parties. Rapport is a "harmonious relationship" between the parties. The friendlier and more cooperative the relationship between the parties, the better the discussions between them. Certainly rapport is not possible in every circumstance—but positive rapport is an important aim that, if achieved, will enhance our opportunities for interviewing success. The absence of rapport, most likely, will result in an undesirable reaction such as apathy, noncooperation, or even antagonism.

Rapport is not a single event or something that happens at a particular instant, but an ongoing process that involves creating and maintaining trust, confidence, and cooperation between the parties. Rapport should be a goal at all times. Probably everyone has met someone they liked immediately and, conversely, has come across someone else they very quickly did not like or trust. Often, these positive feelings or feelings of ill will are based on how the other person acts, on the individual's demeanor, or what the person says.

Most people tend to form judgments quickly, and it sometimes takes a long time for negative feelings to be modified or reversed.

Rapport can also change across time. As stated, many of us have met people we did not initially like or trust. But the more we became acquainted with the other person, the better we liked and trusted them. The opposite also occurs. There are individuals who are very attractive early in a relationship, but the more we get to know them, the less we trust, like, or relate well to them. The same phenomenon can occur in interviewing—sometimes within a single interview and other times across time.

Rapport in interviewing situations begins to develop before or during the first meeting. The interviewer must first project a good impression and gain the respect of the person being interviewed. One goal is to "be attractive," in other words, to project the type of image that will engender trust along with genuine friendliness, honesty, sincerity, and concern. So how can we engender rapport? The answer is multifaceted. But, a good start is made by knowing what we are doing, being open and caring, being sincere, and providing opportunities for good communication to occur. With some people from linguistically or culturally diverse cultures, rapport begins to develop through what some Hispanics call *platicando*, which involves a somewhat brief, casual, and important "warm up" characterized by some preliminary chitchat type of conversation (Langdon, 1992; Sharifzadeh, 1992).

Whenever there is poor rapport, or poor harmony between the other party and ourselves, we need to try to determine if there is something we are doing to disrupt the development and maintenance of rapport. Sometimes it is not the interviewer who is causing the breakdown to occur, but it is wise to first check on ourselves.

6. *Be sensitive and courteous.*

Sensitivity and courtesy are a little different, but often highly related. Being **sensitive** is an earmark of successful interviewers, irrespective of the type of interview conducted. People respond favorably to another person when they feel they are being treated courteously and with respect and when they feel they are being listened to and understood. People tend to "open up" and share important information if they feel they can trust the other person and feel that what they say will be treated appropriately. Part of being sensitive is understanding how much the other person knows about a given subject, that person's comfort with the situation and about the topics of discussion, and that party's abilities to understand and express themselves about a given subject.

Information that we share with another person should be con-veyed respectfully, particularly when the information is negative or distressing (Mowrer, 1988). Individuals and their feelings should be respected, along with their reactions to any information being con-veyed. Sensitivity includes respect for the other party as well as being empathetic to how the other party feels. Fenlason (1962) has commented that being capable of identifying with another person's feelings and actions "is the essence of understanding the 'why' of another's attitudes and behavior" (p. 204). During an interview, the person conducting the interview simultaneously learns about and attempts to understand the other party. Conveying empathy or sympathy, if appropriate, are characteristics of sensitive listeners. Interviewers must also recognize that how other people feel about a subject—whether those feelings are appropriate or inappropriate—will influence how they respond to the subject being discussed.

People appreciate being treated fairly and with dignity. Part of this involves being treated with **courtesy**. There are many factors that go into feelings of being treated courteously: not having to wait long for an appointment, being greeted appropriately, not being inter-rupted when speaking, being allowed to express something of importance, having the other person's undivided attention, being addressed by a preferred name, having questions of concern answered, and much more. A good guideline is for us to treat the other person with the type of courtesy and sensitivity that we would like to receive.

7. *Be aware of interviewees' levels of overall knowledge.*

Someone's general levels of intelligence and education can influ-ence communication in an interview situation. The interviewee's education may come from formal schooling or real-life experience. We all meet people with very little formal education who are very knowledgeable about the subjects of discussion and about life, in general. Conversely, we can meet very highly educated people who know very little about the subjects we are discussing or have very little information outside of their particular area of expertise. The point is not to automatically equate someone's level of formal edu-cation with their overall level of knowledge.

Any interviewee's level of knowledge will be influenced by what they have experienced in life (through real-world experience, formal education, reading, friends, etc.). It is important that we recognize an interviewee's general level of knowledge and tailor our language use accordingly. We cannot automatically assume that another party has the same level of knowledge that we have. Recognition of and sensitivity toward an interviewee's level of knowledge and general intelligence will promote a good working relationship and good communication.

8. *Be aware of interviewees' knowledge about topics of discussion.*

An aspect of sensitivity and courtesy involves understanding the other party's levels of knowledge about the subject areas under discussion. In many cases, the interviewer and interviewee will have considerably different levels of knowledge about an area of discussion. For example, an insurance agent may know a considerable amount about insurance, with the person being interviewed possibly knowing only that insurance exists and might be a good idea. Or, in a professional mental health setting, the interviewer may know a great deal about psychology and how people react to different situations, with the patient having self-knowledge about personal feelings and degrees of unhappiness. In this example, both parties know a good deal of information, but their types of knowledge and levels of this knowledge may be very different.

Interviewers should be very careful to avoid technical jargon or, if they use it, define such terminology immediately in understandable terms. Interviewees cannot follow the interviewer if the terminology goes "over their head." There is an important balance that needs to be achieved; we need to be careful to neither talk over someone else's head nor appear to be talking down to them. Both of these are counterproductive in that they lead to ill feelings. Of course, talking over someone else's head will result in that person not knowing what we are talking about. Talking at a too elementary or too sophisticated level will both engender resentment and hostility.

Let's use an example from the field of medicine. A physician who relays a patient's condition and diagnosis in technical jargon will probably overwhelm the patient rather than inform the person. The patient may leave the interaction confused and feeling that the doctor was insensitive, uncaring, or even arrogant (Enelow & Swisher, 1986). Conversely, the doctor should not simplify language so much that the patient feels talked down to. Age and education should be taken into consideration when relaying information. Using appropriate terms will help maintain rapport and leave the interviewee with a good feeling about the exchange.

9. *Treat all questions asked seriously and respectfully.*

There is a common expression that "there is no such thing as a dumb question." This expression is used by parents, teachers, supervisors, and many others who want to encourage people to ask, rather than not ask, questions that are on their mind. It is not really true that there is no such thing as a dumb question. Indeed, over the years, we have all heard questions that are quite dumb, poorly thought out, or even redundant. However, when interviewing, it is imperative to treat each question as being important and asked sincerely. Remember that even a "dumb" or repetitive question is important to the person who is asking it. All questions should be fielded forthrightly, courteously, and respectfully.

10. *Be spontaneous and minimize the need for checklists.*

There are certain types of standardized interviews in which interviewers must work from a checklist. For example, some companies employ a standard interview with job applicants to ensure that all applicants have an equal opportunity to respond to a predetermined set of questions. Although needed in certain circumstances, such standardized procedures tend to minimize spontaneous discussions between the parties.

Interviewers in other settings do not rely on a standard interview format; rather, they rely on knowledge of their field and their setting, as well as the specific needs of the individuals they interview. Interviewers in these settings work from a general plan of action, but with much more flexibility and, therefore, the ability to be spontaneous. They can deviate from their overall plan by going with the flow and directions of the interview and moving into different directions as needed.

It is our experience that some of the poorest interviews, indeed some of the poorest interviewers, rely too much on checklists for their interviews. A checklist may be necessary in some settings, but it can severely restrict the topics of discussion and flow of an interview. In a very real sense, anyone who relies too much on a checklist is probably someone who only asks questions and records responses, rather than being a really effective interviewer. Good interviews require spontaneity, as these interactions can change directions for any of a number of reasons. For example, the interviewee may have important questions to ask, may not understand some questions that are asked, may think of something new that needs discussing, or the person being interviewed may not respond to a particular line of questioning. The interviewer must take shifts in the interview's direction in stride. Although the interviewer should control the direction of an interview, there must be skill in making appropriate changes as needed throughout the interview.

Among other factors, the abilities to be appropriately spontaneous and flexible seem related to one's personality, knowledge of the field, valid knowledge of personal strengths and weaknesses, and security with self. If interviewers are confident in their knowledge of the subjects of discussion and interviewing and its techniques, they seem better able to handle shifts during interviews. Flexible interviewers can vary their approaches depending on the background and education of the interviewee and the circumstances that occur within an interview. In effect, they can adapt appropriately to a particular party being interviewed.

11. *Recognize differences among people, including age and maturity.*

Just as interviewers have varying backgrounds, philosophies, and cultural influences, interviewees have different personalities, backgrounds, beliefs, and needs. A single type of textbook-like interviewee does not exist. Therefore, interviewers must be prepared to adapt to the variations among the people they will interview and be sensitive to those differences. Rich (1968) noted that communication in an interview may be influenced by various factors. Age, sex, intelligence, cultural background, language skills, educational levels, and the presence of disabilities or specific difficulties can all influence communication and rapport between an interviewer and interviewee. A person conducting an interview may also need to consider the possible influences of the interviewee's family, friends, or even social or religious backgrounds. The conscientious interviewer will realize the importance of a careful analysis of these factors on a case-by-case basis.

Many young interviewers fear that they will not be accepted as being credible because of their age, particularly by clients who are older than them. This can be somewhat true when dealing with some individuals from cultures where age and maturity are highly respected or honored. However, age is only one variable that can often be overcome by demonstrating appropriate respect and sensitivity, being aware of the influences in effect, and being perceived as being knowledgeable and caring (Haynes, Pindzola, & Emerick, 1992; Shipley, 1992).

The following are general comments applicable to interviews with children, adolescents, and older people. There is considerable variability among people within each of these age groupings. Therefore, keep in mind the inherent limitations of generalizations in applying these to individuals. Interviewing children can be difficult for some interviewers, particularly if they have not been around a lot of youngsters. It may be helpful to recognize that:

- Most American children are used to talking with adults even if it is only with their caregivers, family members, babysitters, or teachers.
- Children appreciate and respond to being treated with courtesy and respect. Most youngsters like to be treated as "conversational equals."
- Like adults, children need a "comfort zone" of space. We do not want to violate their space by getting too close, at least initially. Conversely, we do not want to "put off" someone whose space comfort zone is less than ours by reacting to too much closeness. Also, be aware that many children are uncomfortable being touched by strangers or those with whom they have had little previous contact.
- Although children's vocabularies are still developing, they still know a lot about their language and world. Some 2- and 3-year-olds can carry out very "adult" conversations, if we listen and use vocabularies appropriate to their age.
- American children will generally talk openly with adults who listen, suggest topics for discussion, let the child take the lead, and do not act in a judgmental manner. However, some children from linguistically and culturally diverse backgrounds (e.g., some Asian and Native American groups) may have been trained to be silent and respectful in the presence of unfamiliar adults. Such children will need to get to know the adult before really opening up.
- Children will also talk rather openly if they trust the adult. However, violate this trust and you may have a very nontalkative child.

Interviewing adolescents can also present some challenges. It may be helpful to realize that:

- Most teenagers are, in many ways, more like adults than children and they like to be treated accordingly.

- Teenagers are going through a number of changes and pressures that can affect their attitudes and behavior.
- Adolescents, as a group, are under considerable peer pressure; there are conflicting needs both to conform and to be different. What their friends may think can be very important to adolescents. They may deny certain problems or realities just to be like their friends.
- An interviewer being from a different age group is typically not a difficulty, if we can demonstrate concern for the individual while generating trust and credibility.
- A good sense of humor and a tolerant nature can be important assets when dealing with certain adolescents, particularly those who may try to shock, challenge, or discourage the interviewer.
- Rather than trying to act like a teenager, it can be useful to maintain a professional, sincere role to develop and maintain feelings of respect.
- Our competence and concern may be best demonstrated by our words and actions. Adolescents typically appreciate and respect honesty; it is often helpful to honestly describe what is being done and why, as well as our reasoning for the approach. (Partially adapted from Haynes et al., 1992, pp. 19–20.)

Working with older persons might also seem challenging for some youthful interviewers. Writing in the field of medicine, Enelow and Swisher (1986) devote an entire chapter of their book, *Interviewing and Patient Care*, to interviewing the older adult. The following paraphrases part of their work. In reading the listing, be aware that there is considerable variability among older people; all items will not necessarily apply to all individuals who are older.

- Remember that elderly persons grew up in different eras. They will have many experiences (wars, the Great Depression, better times, worse times, etc.) that differ from those of the interviewer. However, these persons are also products of today's society (TV, Fax machines, modern advertising, modern medicine, etc.). Being a part of two different age cultures can make interviewing a challenge.
- The physical setting can be a crucial factor when interviewing older persons. Good lighting, good acoustics, and comfortable seating will facilitate a good interview; poor lighting, a noisy

or distracting environment, and such things as uncomfortable seating or no seating can all adversely affect an interview situation with anyone, but particularly with those who are older.

- Many older people value propriety. Politeness and proper respect may help set them at ease. Also, many older people prefer to be called by their family name rather than their first name. This preference should be honored. It is important when interviewing older adults to first introduce ourselves. This can be particularly important with many individuals from linguistically and culturally diverse cultures.

- Many older people were raised at a time when personal problems were neither discussed openly nor outside the immediate family. For this reason, some older interviewees may be hesitant to answer personal questions about their feelings, medical or psychological issues, or other matters that they believe should stay within oneself or within the immediate family.

- Recognize that the time it takes to respond to a question may increase with age. We may need to be patient with some older interviewees and not push them too quickly for an answer. Sometimes, delays in responding are caused by the physiologic nature of aging; other times, there may simply be a long history that has to be thought out before responding. A 25-year-old, for example, has seen and experienced a lot less than someone who is much older.

- Some elderly interviewees may depend heavily on family members for help and support. Depending on the nature of the interview, an interviewer may want to consider having a family member present during the interview. (Adapted from Enelow & Swisher, 1986, pp. 148–153)

Again, we want to caution that the preceding listings are generalizations that may not apply to particular individuals.

In summary, age can be a factor that influences an interview, particularly if either the interviewer or the party being interviewed is very concerned about it. Age can also be a factor if the interviewer is not sensitive to factors that relate to age differences. However, when an interviewer is knowledgeable, appropriately self-confident, concerned with the matters at hand, and sensitive to the varying needs of interviewees, age does not have to be a significant issue over time. For most parties being interviewed, issues of trust, sincerity, and competence outweigh any age differences.

12. *Recognize that participants' gender can affect interviews.*

Everyone who has passed beyond early infancy is aware that there are differences between males and females. There are physiologic as well as emotional differences. Despite some sexist rhetoric heard from members of both sexes from time to time, there is no better or second best gender—there are just differences. This applies to interviewing in that there are differences in how both genders tend to communicate and interact. Again, this is not good or bad; there are simply differences.

It has been well-documented that there can be differences between interviewees' responses based on whether the interviewer is male or female (see, for example, Burgoon, 1994; Casciani, 1978; Kleinke, 1986; McCroskey, Richmond, & Stewart, 1986). The interviewer's gender may affect his or her approaches to the person being interviewed, as well as wordings used. Conversely, an interviewee may respond differently to questions posed by a member of the same sex than they would to a member of the opposite sex.

The following are several generalities characteristic of the general American culture that must be viewed carefully because there are so many exceptions to any generalization. Given that preface, we do find that females tend to reveal more information about themselves, tend to be more open to discussion, and are generally more expressive than males. Males tend to be more reserved, more guarded, and less verbal than females (Burgoon, 1994; McCroskey et al., 1986). Nonverbally, females exchange more eye contact and exhibit more facial emotion than males. Males are less likely to cry, but are more likely to show feelings such as anger through their facial expression (McCroskey et al., 1986).

Now that we have said that there are differences, it is important to emphasize that neither research nor practical experience suggest that either sex makes better interviewers. Similarly, there is no evidence to suggest that either sex is particularly easier or better to interview, although culture can play a role in interviewing. For example, among some Muslims, it would be inappropriate for a male interviewer to be alone in a room with a female interviewee. Another person, preferably a family member, should also be in the room (Nellum-Davis, 1993).

13. *Recognize that culture has a powerful influence on people.*

The area of culture has been alluded to several times in our discussions. Cultural background is a powerful factor that is always present within people (Fenlason, 1962). One's culture, at both conscious and subconscious levels, has a deep influence on a person's thoughts, attitudes, and actions. Cultures differ in interactive patterns, views of the world, what is deemed right and wrong, what should or should not be done, what is important, how time is viewed, the family structure, and in many more ways. Realize that no culture is inherently better or worse than any other; each culture and subculture is just different. And the members of a particular culture are a product of and part of that culture.

Interviewers working with people from different cultures need a strong grounding in cultural relativity and knowledge about the particular cultures of their clients. Understanding the mores and values of a culture helps an interviewer understand the interviewee's responses and attitudes. Even if the interviewer does not have a full understanding and appreciation of the other culture, respect for the beliefs and basic characteristics of that culture in needed.

14. *Understand the role of family and friends.*

With very rare exceptions, people do not live in isolation but within and around others. We function as part of something rather than being operators "within a vacuum" or in isolation. Family and friends often play a large role in shaping a person's attitudes. Depending on the subject of an interview, family or friends can have powerful impacts—positively or negatively—on how interviewees perceive the topics of an interview and how they interact with an interviewer. For example, the interviewee may receive support and encouragement regarding the interview itself or topics to be discussed within an interview, which provide motivation to help ensure a successful interview. On the other hand, an interviewee who is teased by peers, or is discouraged to participate by family members, may participate or cooperate much less freely. One might even encounter resistance or absolute noncooperation. In some instances, the help and cooperation of others in the interviewee's environment might be needed for success.

The role of family varies across different cultures. The general American culture tends to value independence and individualism, whereas the Pacific Islander, Asian, Native American, and Hispanic cultures tend to more emphasize the role of family (Marin & Marin, 1991; Roseberry-McKibbin, 1995). Thus, more family involvement, as opposed to one-to-one involvement, may be necessary and appropriate with some individuals from culturally and linguistically diverse backgrounds.

15. *Strive to increase personal knowledge.*

Years ago, DeBlassie (1976) wrote that one characteristic of effective counselors is wisdom. Knowledge and wisdom are important for most interviewers. Interviewers should certainly be knowledgeable about their chosen field. Likewise, it can be very helpful to have an understanding of the world as a whole. To relate to various cultures, beliefs, and different types of people, the interviewer should work to increase knowledge about the world, in general. It can be helpful to be up-to-date on current events, what is happening in the world, current trends and forces, and how people are similar and different. This certainly helps broaden the base of interviewers' knowledge and abilities to communicate with others.

Minimally, effective interviewers are well-versed in their chosen field. Few people would want a doctor to practice medicine today based on information available even 10 or 15 years ago. The same is true in fields dealing with technology, educational systems, health care provision, investment strategies, and so forth. Effective, up-to-date interviewers actively seek out new information about their field on an ongoing basis.

CHAPTER
3

Basic Suggestions for Effective Interviews

An interview can be a positive experience for both the person conducting the interview and the party being interviewed, with a strong working relationship developed and valuable information exchanged. An interview can also be a negative experience between two parties, causing misunderstandings or ill feelings between the participants. There are many factors that contribute to an interaction being positive or negative—effective or ineffective. The information in this chapter provides basic suggestions to help bolster the opportunities for a good interview situation. Areas addressed include preparation for interviews, providing an appropriate environment for interviews, dressing appropriately, punctuality and timeliness, and recordkeeping of interviews.

1. *Be prepared and organized for interviews.*

The preparation for an interview is a very important factor in its eventual success. Before conducting an interview, "homework" needs to be done. Part of this homework is being knowledgeable about interviewing as well as the subject areas that might be discussed in a particular interview. Without knowledge within either of these areas, we invite less than desired results. The interviewer should have a clearly defined purpose in mind and a plan for achieving that purpose. When taking a long road trip into unfamiliar territory, we cannot expect to just get into the car, start driving, and arrive at the desired destination without at least receiving good directions from someone or using a road map. Likewise, it is unwise to expect to achieve the goals of a particular interview without having some form of a road map in mind. Minimally, we need to contemplate what we need to do in the interview and how we will do it.

Whereas preparing for an interview is an absolute necessity, interviewers should understand that unexpected changes occur during interviews. Rarely does an interview go exactly as we may have planned. People being interviewed often have special concerns or questions they would like addressed or they might even feel uncomfortable with a certain line of questioning or the topics being posed. To maintain rapport, effective interviewers adapt the interview to the needs and concerns of the person being interviewed. This does not mean that interviewers should relinquish control of the interaction. Rather, the interviewer needs to remain in control of the interview while allowing flexibility for different concerns to be addressed and different directions to be taken.

Whether or not we actually write them down, we should be able to list the major points or topics that need to be discussed beforehand. It is also helpful to consider the "what ifs" we could encounter. For example, what if the customer says it's too expensive? What if the caregiver does not know the child's medical history? What if the interviewee disagrees with the diagnosis?

All materials, files, or other forms of information that might be needed should be available and easy to locate. This saves embarrassment, frustration, or appearing unprepared or disorganized and avoids wasting time if certain items cannot be readily located.

2. *Arrange the setting for comfort and communication.*

The outcome of an interview can be influenced by the setting in which the interview takes place (McCroskey et al., 1986; Moursund, 1993). A comfortable setting promotes good communication and rapport. The physical setting should be arranged to ensure communication and privacy. First impressions count; make sure the setting appears comfortable, private, and as if someone cares.

Moursund (1985) has stated that interviewees' first introductions to a setting begin with their visual impressions of the setting. A setting and its atmosphere can put clients at ease or evoke concern or nervousness. The location, furniture, color scheme, sounds, and smells all influence the interviewee's feelings about a setting and, therefore, the interviewer. These first impressions influence interviewees' thinking about the services provided and even the professionalism of the person conducting the interview. For example, Terrell and Terrell (1993) discussed the role of music in waiting rooms with African American patients. They noted that background music is presumed to serve an important function by helping those who are waiting to relax. "Most professional offices play classical or popular easy-listening music. Not only does this music not relax many African Americans, but it also makes them feel uncomfortable, since it makes them feel out of place" (p. 7). They suggest that, when serving African American clients, it may be better to consider playing jazz, which is a more universally accepted form of music.

The setting should be clean, pleasant, and free of distractions. We want people to focus on the discussions at hand—not noticing water stains on the ceiling, how dirty the room is, that there are folders everywhere, a leftover lunch, and so forth. Even the worst possible place can be helped if kept clean and brightened up with a few decorations like plants and pictures. McCroskey et al. (1986) commented that:

> Research indicates that when placed in any ugly room, people become discontented, irritable, bored, fatigued, and generally want out of the environment. Conversely, people placed in attractive surroundings work harder, are less fatigued, communicate more, are less irritable, and do not mind remaining in the setting for a reasonable period of time. (p. 135)

Clearly, it is vital for the setting to be pleasant.

It is also important that the client is within a comfortable proximity to the interviewer. The physical seating arrangements and the distance between the parties are, indeed, factors in interviewing. There is a considerable amount of research in interviewing and counseling to support that seating arrangements and distances between the participants should be considered carefully rather than just happening by chance (see, for example, Benjamin, 1981; Edinburg, Zinberg, & Kelman, 1975; McCroskey et al., 1986). No one particular seating arrangement is clearly superior to all others, but one arrangement that is typically more comfortable and productive than others is with the participants seated somewhat close together at a 90° angle to each other with a small table between them (Benjamin, 1981; Riley, 1972). This arrangement is somewhat non-threatening because of the table between the parties. It also allows either party to look directly at the other person, or to avoid eye contact by looking straight ahead.

The distance separating participants during the interview has been discussed by many authorities (e.g., Cormier & Hackney, 1987; Mehrabian, 1972; Smith, 1973). A smaller distance between people conveys an atmosphere of more intimate communication.

Greater distances are perceived as being less intimate and more formal (Mehrabian, 1968).

Individuals have a specifically defined "bubble," which is their personal space. The size of this bubble varies with culture, environment, gender, age, and familiarity with the other party (see Burgoon, 1994; Hall, 1964; Kleinke, 1986; McCroskey et al., 1986). People choose whom they allow into their bubble; close friends can get closer, with new acquaintances usually kept at a greater distance. Entering a personal bubble without permission hampers communication and rapport. Interviewers should try to determine each interviewee's personal space needs and respect this distance (Hall, 1964). In the Anglo American culture, a distance of 3 to 4 feet between the parties is generally appropriate. Less space or extreme distance both can inhibit effective communication (Cormier & Hackney, 1987; Roberts & Bouchard, 1989).

The following are some general observations concerning distance:

- Women tend to use less distance than men.
- Somewhere between 4 and 8 years of age, children adopt adult-like space norms. Prior to that time, spatial requirements may vary considerably among children.
- People who know each other and have established a relationship use less space between them than people who are just beginning a relationship.
- Distances between parties during interviews are, in part, culturally related. For instance, people of Latin American, Italian, and Puerto Rican descent tend to use less space when talking. On the other hand, people of German, Chinese, Japanese, or Caucasian American extraction are generally more comfortable with greater distances when communicating.
- People who have a large degree of status and authority tend to feel comfortable interacting from less distance. People with less status tend to want more space (Shipley, 1992; Sue, 1988).

There will be many exceptions to these generalities. It is important for the interviewer to observe the preference of the interviewee. Ensuring appropriate distances will facilitate comfort and good communication during an interview.

3. *Provide a private, confidential setting.*

Privacy is an important factor in an effective interview, particularly if any types of personal or potentially sensitive information are discussed. An interviewee will be less apt to share information if there is the possibility of being overheard by others or if there are interruptions. Working to ensure privacy and being attentive to the interviewee are critical to a good working relationship (Donaghy, 1990; Rae, 1988; Shertzer & Stone, 1980).

The interviewee should be made to feel important. Disruptions, such as phone calls, should be avoided whenever possible (Benjamin, 1981; Samovar & Hellweg, 1982). Allowing interviews to be interrupted can make persons being interviewed feel that the interviewer does not value their time or is preoccupied with other matters. If the session is interrupted for the interviewer to conduct other forms of business, the interviewee may feel that they are in the way. The result may be bad feelings that hamper communication.

Privacy is affected by the physical structure of the interview environment. In many professions, it is both unethical and impractical to conduct an interview in an environment where privacy cannot be ensured. Obviously, private matters should not be discussed within earshot of others. The interviewer's work environment should ensure adequate privacy for the interview and all written material pertaining to the interview.

4. Dress appropriately.

The interviewee's first impression of the person conducting the interview is as important as their first impression of the setting. The interviewer should be well-groomed and, in almost all cases, appear professional. Most authorities suggest that the interviewer dress conservatively to convey a professional appearance. Meier and Davis (1993) comment that the dress of the interviewer becomes a problem if it calls attention to itself. Kleinke (1986) states that most people prefer that interviewers dress formally enough to maintain an image of expertise, but not so formally that they appear stuffy or inapproachable.

The appearance of an interviewer should evoke respect and trust. Interviewees often make judgments at the beginning of an interview about the abilities and demeanor of the interviewer, as well as the degrees of respect being conveyed by the interviewer. These impressions will either promote rapport and communication—or negatively influence the interview. Thus, dressing appropriately is a factor in influencing how the other party feels about the interviewer and, therefore, it can affect the communication that occurs between them.

5. *Be punctual and use time wisely.*

Another detail that influences the outcome of interviews is the interviewer's punctuality and management of time. The time available for an interview and the way that time is managed can affect interviews (McCroskey et al., 1986; Samovar & Hellweg, 1982). The interviewee should be told the length of time an interaction is expected to take. This estimate of time will likely, of course, be approximate rather than an absolutely precise commitment. Although adhering to a schedule, the interviewer should appear to have adequate time for the interviewee's questions and concerns.

The time required for an interview will vary depending on the nature of an interview, how verbal the participants are, and the purposes that need to be accomplished. However, interviews that last longer than 45 to 60 minutes are typically exhausting and often become nonproductive (Enelow & Swisher, 1986; Garrett, 1982). If an interview does exceed 45 to 60 minutes, it may be wise to take a break or to resume discussions at another time. Another meeting can usually be scheduled to complete any unfinished business (Benjamin, 1981).

An important aspect of time management is promptness (Dillard & Reilly, 1988; Meier, 1989). Negative feelings often develop if one party is late to the interview. The interviewer must regard the other party's time as being valuable and make every effort to be on time. In the general American culture, if the interviewer begins an interview any more than a few minutes late, the interviewee may already be somewhat irritated and not particularly pleased with the interviewer. This agitation can certainly influence the interaction. Interviewers should be on schedule for appointments and not assume that their time is more valuable than their interviewees' time. Time and its importance does vary across cultures, so interviewers need to understand the cultural values of time relevance across varying groups and individuals.

6. *Keep appropriate records.*

Attention should not be focused on record keeping during an interview (Garrett, 1982). Rather, the emphasis during the interaction should be on putting the person being interviewed at ease, encouraging that person to communicate openly, guiding the discussion appropriately, listening carefully, observing, and interpreting body language and underlying meanings. But some form of record keeping needs to be completed in most interviewing situations. At the very least, such records usually indicate who was interviewed, the date and approximate times, the areas of discussion, any conclusions reached, and an indication of any future follow-up needed.

Note taking is one way of recording information gained during an interview. However, taking notes should not detract from the flow of the interaction (Benjamin, 1981; Okun, 1987). When taking notes, these should be taken openly and not hidden from the interviewee. Taking notes in a secretive manner can engender mistrust and negative feelings.

There are several positive aspects to note taking. Some interviewees view an interviewer's note taking as having a genuine interest in their particular situation; in effect, what they are saying is being heard and noted. For interviewers, the process allows them to rather precisely record what the interviewee has said. This becomes a good reference point for future use and to refresh the memory.

Some form of note taking is probably beneficial within most interviews. However, note taking should never be so detailed that it forces an interviewer to miss important parts of the interview— whether these missed portions are verbal or nonverbal. Note taking should not disrupt the flow of an interview and should not dictate the pace or focus of the interaction. Also, note taking should not be used as an "escape" or "cop-out" preventing free interaction with the other person. People who are overly concerned with their note taking are not interacting in a communicative, give-and-take fashion with the other party.

For most interview situations, the best form of note taking is to record brief notes of the major points during the conversation. Then, immediately following the interview, to take a few moments to review the session and write more detailed notes. This allows us to make the notes while our memory is still fresh and enables us to determine the most important points that need to be recorded. This cannot be done as effectively during the interaction.

An accurate record of an interview is also possible through audio- or videotape recording. A detailed and accurate record of an interview can be recorded and evaluated, either immediately following the meeting or at a future date. Audio- and videotaping an interview is usually permissible with prior approval of the person being interviewed; for ethical and possibly legal reasons it should not be done secretly. Also be aware that interactive patterns and what is actually said—by either the interviewing or interviewed party—can be adversely affected in the recording process. People tend to be more guarded and communicate "closer to the vest" when being recorded.

7. *Avoid checklist interviews.*

Some interviewers use a checklist of questions or question areas as a basis for their interviewing. A checklist is one way to ensure that the interview follows a desired course and addresses the major items that need to be discussed. Usually employed for information-getting interviews, questions are listed on a form that can be followed during the interaction. A checklist interview can be useful when there are only a few major items that need to be addressed and a pure "questions and answers" format will accomplish the purposes of the interview. There are, however, some problems with this type of interview. The most important problem is that it tends to involve the asking of a question, getting a specific response, asking another question, getting another response, and so forth. Such an interview can be pretty superficial and noninteractive. Also, this format does not allow for give-and-take between the participants— there is little opportunity to move into areas that are not listed on the questionnaire and the whole interaction can appear pretty superficial or robot-like with checklists. The interviewer may be so focused with the questions on the list, or on writing down the interviewee's responses, that other important information is missed, such as feelings, nonverbal reactions, or other forms of body language.

Overreliance on checklists is seen at times in beginning interviewers, or with interviewers who are insecure about interviewing, in general. In most instances, it is far better for interviewers to be familiar with the questions they need to ask and to engage in a more natural, conversational approach. If needed, a brief listing of the major items that need to be discussed can be used—but for use as a reference rather than as an overused tool.

CHAPTER
4

Structuring Interviews

Good interviews do not just happen. They result from having a specific purpose, preparation, a plan of action, knowledge, and the skillful use of appropriate techniques. Interviews are structured to optimize our chances for success. There are three distinct segments, or phases, within interviews: an opening, the body of the interview, and a closing. There are specific types of information contained within each of these phases. The use of these phases helps interviewers organize an interview and promotes the opportunities for success. Several factors that affect success, including the basic structure for interviews, are discussed in this chapter.

1. *Determine the basic purpose of the interview and structure it accordingly.*

In Chapter 1, we said that any interview should have a specific purpose. There is really no reason to conduct an interview unless we know precisely why we need it. This purpose determines the type of interview conducted. Let's use an example with a teacher:

- If there is a need to find out about a child and how that child is doing at home, the teacher can conduct a conference. The conference is essentially an **information-getting interview**.
- If the teacher needs to share information about how a child is doing in school, then the conference would be an **information-giving interview**.
- Now let's assume that the child is falling asleep in class and reports being up very late at night. Our teacher might call a

conference to try to persuade the caregiver to pay more attention to the child's bedtime and needs for rest. This would be an **influencing, persuasive, or counseling interview**.

Examples can be drawn from almost any profession: law, medicine and health-related services, mental health, sales, management, finances, personnel, and so forth. Virtually any interviewing activity can fall within one of the three categories just detailed.

Clearly the purpose of an interview will determine the type of interview conducted and the role of the interviewer will be different within each type. This role may be collecting information; providing information; influencing, persuading, or counseling; or even some combination of these. However, each of the three types will have the same structure, namely:

- An opening phase
- The body of the interview, and
- A closing phase.

What goes into each phase will be a little different in each type of interview. This is discussed a little later on in the chapter. Right now, let's focus on preparing for an interview.

2. *Ready yourself for the interview.*

We discussed being prepared and organizing for interviewing in Chapter 3. Closer to the actual interview, one may want to:

- Make sure any appropriate background material is known, whether it is a child's performance in school, the law related to a client's case, a medical history, the product or service being sold, or whatever. One simply needs to know what one is talking about.
- Determine specifically what one is trying to do. Is one trying to discover a client's financial needs, parents' concerns about their child's progress in school, or someone's medical history? Is one trying to describe different options for solving some problem? Or is one trying to encourage or convince someone to do something? Note that these three examples illustrate an information-getting, information-giving, and influencing, persuasive, or counseling types of interviews.
- Develop an approach or course of action. Determine what needs to be addressed, how it will be addressed, and in what order.

- Understand that there are two parties in every interview, that we may need to deal with objective and subjective types of information, that there will probably be digressions during the discussion, and that one or both parties may have apprehensions and concerns before and during the interview. It is also possible, depending on how well the interview goes, the subjects discussed, and the parties' reactions to these topics, that there may be apprehension or concern after the interview is over.
- Prepare the physical environment, such as gathering anything that will be needed, putting unnecessary items away, straightening the furniture, and so forth.

3. Orient the interviewee.

Orienting an interviewee means providing information that will prepare the interviewee for the interaction. We can help prepare an interviewee for what to expect in a number of ways. This is important because a tentative relationship between an interviewer and interviewee starts to develop even before their first meeting (Moursund, 1993). For interviewers, any information they learn about their interviewee can lead to certain preliminary impressions about that person. This can include feelings about the party being interviewed, and what some of that party's needs or attitudes might be. On the other hand, interviewees' perceptions about the reputation of the interviewer, the appearance and location of the setting, and the purpose of an interview can affect interviewees' initial attitudes and behavior.

Presession orientations (occurring before the interview itself) set the stage for a successful interview. They alert the person being interviewed to the basic purposes of the interview, generally what to expect, and approximately how long the interview will take. There are several ways to provide interviewees with presession orientations directly or even indirectly through an interpreter when this is appropriate. In a setting with support staff, a receptionist can provide general information about the interviewer, any fees charged, basic procedures, and the approximate length of the interview. The support staff responsible for handling such information will, of course, need to be trained to provide appropriate information to interviewees, their families, or others acting on their behalf.

Presession orientations can also be accomplished by direct contact with the parties. This is typically handled by telephone with the interviewee given the opportunity to speak briefly with the person conducting the interview before the first meeting. Another way for an interviewer to orient the person being interviewed is by sending written information. Written information may be a letter or pamphlet describing the facility or basic information about the products or services involved. An appointment card with other introductory material is used in some settings. Of course, any written materials should be in the language most comfortable for the client, as the purpose is to expedite communication and facilitate a good working relationship. In summary, presession orientations give an interviewee the opportunity for mental preparation for an exchange and "a feel" for the person conducting the interview and any products or services involved.

The title or description someone uses or is referred to also acts to orient the other party. For example, Gelso and Karl (1974) found that students judged counselors' skill levels differently based on the title a counselor used, in effect, what the person was called. Indeed, what someone is called does convey different impressions, at least initially. This is one reason we now see titles like sales counselors or sales representatives rather than salesman or saleswoman or terms like associates rather than employees in many settings. Because different titles imply varying levels of credibility, experience, or expertise, it is important to consider how we are referred to carefully. Any job title should be accurate, convey what we do, and be understandable to the consumer. Personal references should also be considered carefully: first name or last name, or Dr., Mr., Miss, Mrs., or Ms. Many clients, particularly some who are older or come from linguistically or culturally diverse groups, will be more comfortable with greater degrees of formality.

4. *Use an opening to establish rapport and provide further orientation.*

There are three stages, or phases, to an interview: an opening, the body, and a closing. The opening phase of an interview introduces the interview and gets it off to an appropriate beginning. This phase orients the clients to what will be discussed and, as such, sets the stage for the discussions that will follow. The opening phase of an interview is somewhat like the opening of a television show. TV writers know that the opening of a show is critical; it will either capture the viewer's attention and interest or the viewer is likely to switch channels. Similarly, the opening of an interview will capture the other party's initial interest and attention—or it will fail to do so.

The differences are typically in how the interviewer begins the interview in this opening phase. A good opening provides orientation for the interviewee, gives an overview of the basic areas of discussion, and helps establish rapport between the parties (Stewart & Cash, 1994).

When both the interviewer and the interviewee know what to expect from the exchange, rapport can develop rather quickly. The orientation in the opening phase of the interview provides this information. During the opening phase, the interviewer briefly defines the roles of the participants and indicates some of the specific activities that will occur (Haynes et al., 1992).

The opening phase of an interview can be structured through the interviewer's introduction, a brief role description, and statement of the purpose of the interview. In most settings, it is wise for the person conducting the interview to note or reiterate the specific purpose of the interview or the nature of the information that will be discussed (Peterson & Marquardt, 1994). It is also helpful to tell the interviewee how any information obtained will be used, why it is needed, and to whom it may or may not be revealed. Finally, the interviewee is told approximately how long the interview will take.

Some interviewers employ just a little small talk during the opening phase; others do not. These brief periods of small talk do not relate directly to the purpose of the interview, but sometimes help "break the ice." Too much small talk at the beginning can be distressing to certain interviewees and wastes valuable time. However, some period of brief chitchat is important to many persons, particularly with some people from linguistically and culturally diverse cultures. Conversation can help two parties begin to relate with each other before actually getting down to business.

The person conducting an interview should offer a brief, general orientation statement about what will be discussed. In an information-getting interview this statement could be:

> Joe, I've looked over your credentials and you seem to have some good experience. There are several areas of your experience and previous jobs that I need to discuss with you. This will take approximately 20 minutes.

> Mrs. Smith, I understand you haven't been feeling well lately. To understand the problems, I need you to tell me about your symptoms. Then I'll do an examination. We should be finished with everything in about a half hour.

In both examples, the interviewee is told in general terms what to expect during the exchange and approximately when the exchange should be finished. As indicated in Chapter 1, rapport should be developed and maintained from the initial to the final contact between the parties in an interview. Rapport is an important consideration for all interviewees, particularly early in relationships (Ivey, 1983).

5. *Make a transition from the opening to the body of the interview.*

The opening phase of an interview is typically brief and aimed at orienting interviewees to whom they are talking with, what they will be talking about, and approximately how long an exchange will take. The body of the interview is where the important information is discussed. With **information-getting interviews**, the transition from the opening to the body of the interview occurs when the first piece of information is requested by the interviewer. For example:

- Tell me what brought you here today.
- Why do you think you'd like to work here?
- What types of information do you need to learn more about?
- What seems to be wrong with your arm?

The interviewee should be encouraged to provide an opening statement of the problem or situation. An open-ended question or comment is often preferred to elicit this, such as "tell me about _____" or "What brought you here today?" Such open-ended stimuli allow interviewees to respond in a number of ways, allowing insight into both their areas of major interest and how strongly they feel about these areas. If, however, the interviewee seems either reluctant to talk or uncertain where to begin, a closed-ended question to elicit specific information might be asked to help the person get started. Closed-ended stimuli are discussed in Chapter 5.

During the body of an interview, the interviewer gains information deemed necessary, provides information, or tries to influence, persuade, or counsel the other party. The structure of the body of the interview is determined by the task (or tasks) to be accomplished. If the purpose of the interview is **information getting**, the person conducting the interview will have specific questions that need to be asked. These questions should be organized to provide continuity within each inquiry area. Jumping back and forth to different topics can confuse an interviewee and might result in some potentially important questions not getting asked.

Also, with **information-giving interviews**, structure may be determined by the interviewee's levels of anxiousness or concern. A transition between the opening and body of the information-giving interview is made in sharing the first piece of information with the other party (e.g., "Based on our analysis, _____"). However, before sharing any information, it is useful to estimate the interviewee's general anxiety levels to decide on how to sequence the information. Typically, with highly anxious or highly concerned interviewees, the overall conclusion (the bottom line) is given at the beginning of the body of the interview. Once interviewees have heard this bottom line, they are likely to be more attentive to the details that led to the conclusion. Less anxious interviewees, however, are typically given the major points or findings first and the ultimate conclusion (or bottom line) last. With the less anxious interviewee, the interviewer may need to "build the case" toward the bottom-line conclusion shared.

The reasoning for this is illustrated by considering a student who has not done well on a term paper. If the student is highly concerned about the grade for the paper, this person may hear very little of the instructor's feedback or constructive suggestions on the paper until the bottom line—the grade—is shared. Only by sharing the bottom line (the grade) first can the student then focus on the other items (misspellings, poor grammar, or whatever) that need to be discussed. Conversely, with an unconcerned or less anxious student, the instructor may need to first point out various problems, thus "building the case" for the bottom-line conclusion.

With **information-getting interviews**, the body includes discussion of whatever information is necessary to understand the case, the situation, or the interviewee's needs. However, the body of **information-giving interviews** is usually limited to sharing the most important results, findings, conclusions, or recommendations. Although more may be known, it is often advisable to limit information shared to the most important items. Three to five major points is a good rule of thumb, but there may be more or less, depending on the situation (Shipley, 1992). By limiting information shared to major points that need to be conveyed, an interviewee is helped in focusing on and truly understanding the major items. Distilling topics covered also helps interviewers to determine the points that are really important and which items are of less importance.

It has been said that "anything worth saying should be said at least three times." This is certainly true when providing information, particularly with sensitive or technical topics. Just because something is said once or even more than once, does not mean that it was heard, let alone understood. The interviewer should repeat the major points several times, varying the wording each time.

The same principles apply to **influencing, persuasive, or counseling interviews**. Sometimes the recommendations are shared first, followed up by items or factors that led to the conclusions or recommendations. Other times, a case that leads to the bottom-line conclusions or suggestions is built. In either case, it's vital for the interviewer to be certain that the other party understands the bottom-line conclusions or recommendations, along with the reasons that support such recommendations or conclusions. Understanding all aspects can help the other party see the need for any actions or changes being suggested. To accomplish this, the number of areas addressed is usually limited, so the interviewee is not overwhelmed or confused.

Irrespective of the type of interview being conducted, it is important to take the time necessary to do the job well. It is also important that the other party feel the process is not being rushed or ill feelings can develop, often very quickly. This occurs across many cultures. As one example, some Native Americans who sense that interviewers are hurried may not discuss certain concerns they have (Anderson & Fenichel, 1989). It is, therefore, important to allot appropriate time for the interview, and give the impression of having such time, so people do not feel rushed.

6. *Close the interview concisely.*

Once the interviewer feels that the purpose of the interview has been achieved, the interview is brought to a close. Interviewers who are less skillful often appear awkward at this point. It is as though everything has been said and they don't know what else to say so they might as well stop, but are unsure quite how to do so. A structured closing prevents such awkwardness and closes the interview in an appropriate, organized fashion. The closing phase of an interview is rather brief. It includes:

- Summarizing the major points that have been discussed.
- Providing the opportunity for interviewees to clarify any inaccurate parts of our summary and providing opportunities to ask any further questions.
- Expressing appreciation to our interviewees. This may include appreciation for their time, interest, candor, efforts, the information provided, or whatever else is appropriate.

- An indication of any further activities or actions, now or in the future, that will be necessary.

These four mechanisms are appropriate for closing all interview types: information-getting, information-giving, and influencing, persuasive, or counseling formats. Reviewing the major points discussed provides a final summary of information obtained in an information-getting interview and helps highlight the major points discussed in information-giving or influencing, persuasive, counseling interviews. These summaries also help interviewees focus on the major points that have been addressed, while helping trigger any further questions they have. The goal is to have as many questions as possible answered before the interviewee leaves; the closing is the final chance for such questions to be asked. The interviewer should avoid introducing any new information in the closing phase, but should address any new questions or concerns the interviewee may have.

Interviewees should be thanked for their time. People lead busy lives and their time is valuable. The final part of the closing phase is to make arrangements for any follow-up interviews or activities needed. People want to know what will occur next and, at least approximately, when it will happen.

The closing of an interview should be rather brief when compared to the more-extensive information covered within the body of the interview, but it should include an accurate summary of the major points discussed. A good closing leaves both parties feeling that the interview has been well handled and that the major information necessary has been covered. Both parties are also aware of future courses of action—in effect, what will happen next.

7. *Record any necessary notes and evaluate the interview.*

After an interview has been completed, any notes needed are completed. It is also beneficial to at least briefly self-evaluate the interview. What was done well? What should have been done differently? Were the main points focused on? Were the interviewee's questions addressed? Was what was needed accomplished and, if not, why? Did the interviewee seem to understand what needs to be done next? These are just a few possible self-evaluation questions that can be asked.

In some settings, and particularly for new interviewers, audio- or videotape recording of sessions allows evaluation of the receptivity of the persons interviewed, interviewer listening and response skills, as well as use of different interviewing techniques. There are a number of methods and checklists that can be used to evaluate specific activities and behaviors that occur within interviewing and counseling sessions. Such checklist systems have been reported by Amidon (1965), Erickson (1950), Hackney and Cormier (1994), Ivey (1994), McDonald and Haney (1988), Molyneaux and Lane (1982), Shipley (1992), and others.

It has been said that experience is the best teacher. Observing successful interviewers in action, practicing specific techniques, gaining experience, and carefully reviewing personal interviewing experiences helps refine our skills, learn to use various techniques effectively, identify and remedy mistakes, and simply become more skilled across time. Becoming more skilled happens with hard work; it does not simply occur. Let's consider this by examining the fallacy that experience simply means the number of years that someone does something. One person with 15 years of experience has continued to develop, refine skills, and truly become much more effective across time and experience. Conversely, another person has simply continued to do the same thing repeatedly and has not really developed further. The first person has 15 years of experience; the second person really has a year's worth of skill that has been repeated 14 more times. The point is that growth and personal development take openness and effort, which result in becoming a more skilled interviewer.

CHAPTER
5

Working with Questions

The primary methods of obtaining information in information-getting interviews are asking questions, listening carefully to the responses, asking follow-up questions, then asking questions within these or other areas of potential importance. Skill is needed in asking appropriate questions and to understand and work effectively with the information resulting from the questions. Listening skills and the types of listening were discussed in Chapter 2. It is important to reiterate the value of listening effectively. Effective listening helps the interviewer interpret and evaluate interviewees' responses, plus determine if follow-up questions are needed, what types of questions should be asked, and even how to frame these questions.

Questions are used by the interviewer to elicit new information, clarify statements made by the person being interviewed, help motivate open communication, and direct the focus of an exchange (Brammer, 1993; Garrett, 1982). There are a number of valid uses of questions by interviewers. However, as Garrett (1982) has pointed out, questions should not be asked simply out of curiosity. There should be a legitimate reason for every question asked. Therefore, it is important for interviewers to understand both their rationale and motive for asking any question.

There are three major types of questions that occur within interviews. These are:

- Open and closed questions,
- Primary and secondary questions, and

- Neutral or leading questions (Stewart & Cash, 1994).

People's responses to these question categories are very different, so it is important to understand the categories—and the type of questions that occur within the categories.

1. *Understand the different types of questions and the kinds of responses each produces.*

Open- and closed-ended questions or directives refer to how "open" or "closed" the question or directive is and, therefore, the type of response that is generated. Open-ended comments, directives, or questions tend to produce relatively long responses in which the interviewee can pick from a variety of possible responses. For example, the directive, "Tell me about your concerns," or the question, "What brought you in today?" are very open; people could respond with a number of possible answers and their responses will typically be more than just a few words. Contrast this with closed-ended stimuli, such as "What is your name?" "Tell me how old you are," "Who did you vote for in the last election?" or "What grade are you in?" These closed-ended questions allow little option for how to respond and typically result in short answers about specifically requested types of information. Thus, open-ended stimuli produce relatively long responses about a wide variety of potential topics. Closed-ended stimuli typically elicit shorter responses about specific topics contained within the questions or directives (Schulman, 1991; Shipley, 1992; Stewart & Cash, 1994).

Primary and secondary questions are either initial (primary) requests for information or follow-up (secondary) requests for information. Primary questions introduce a topic area, being the first question asked within some area. This is contrasted with secondary questions, which are follow-up questions to the primary question asked. Often, a primary question is asked, followed by one or more follow-up, or secondary, questions. Once adequate information about the area of inquiry is obtained, another primary question can be asked to introduce the next area for discussion. This may be followed by asking follow-up secondary questions, and so on. Secondary questions are important for allowing interviewers to "dig into" areas of importance. Information from secondary questions helps the "whole picture" to emerge.

The third category relates to whether or not bias, intentionally or unintentionally, is introduced by the wording of a question or the tone in which it is conveyed. **Leading** questions, by their very nature, can inject bias into responses we get. For example, the classic biased question, "Do you still beat your wife?" presumes that someone's wife has been abused. The question is not whether this ever happened, but whether it is still happening. Questions with bias can lead to biased answers. Sometimes this is appropriate, such as when we are attempting to "sell" an idea or product. Other times, such as when taking certain histories, it is inappropriate because we want genuine responses, unbiased by leading questions. This requires **neutral** questions that do not contain bias in their wording or how they are asked.

2. *Use open questions to stimulate relatively long responses about a wide range of possible topics.*

Open questions are general, relatively nonspecific questions that give the interviewee a wide range of possible responses. In an employment interview, the employer may ask the applicant, "Why would you make a good employee?" The applicant may respond by giving educational background, experience, "people skills," or even desire to work in the particular firm or within certain areas of work responsibility. By using open questions, the interviewer controls the general topic area while allowing the respondent to select what areas are addressed within the responses. Open questions allow interviewees some degree of control over the areas of discussion, what to emphasize, and how much detail to provide.

Open-ended questions must be framed so the respondent cannot respond with a "yes/no" answer or a short response. The object is to draw out as much information as possible about a topic from the interviewee. An interviewer begins an open stimulus with phrases such as, "What are _____?" or "Tell me about _____," for example, "Tell me about some of your concerns" or "What are some of the reasons you came in today?" A form of somewhat open-ended verbalization, sometimes called an **encourager**, involves repeating a respondent's key words.

> **Patient:** I've really been feeling under the weather lately.
> **Doctor:** Under the weather?
>
> **Customer:** My car is making a strange sound.
> **Mechanic:** Strange sound? Tell me about it.

Open-ended questions have several advantages. They tend to elicit information that is more accurate and thought out than responses given to closed questions (Enelow & Swisher, 1986). They also tend to:

- Allow and even encourage interviewee participation,
- Provide opportunities for the interviewer to communicate interest in the respondent,
- Provide more than one response option for the interviewee,
- Reveal the issues that the interviewee feels are most important,
- Allow respondents to provide information that might not have been addressed otherwise,
- Provide insight into the interviewee's knowledge about the topic at hand,
- Reveal topics of interest and concern to the interviewee, and
- Reveal the respondent's prejudices and attitudes. (Adapted from Stewart & Cash, 1994, p. 64)

Open-ended questions do have some disadvantages. They can become very time-consuming, because the answers tend to be long. Some interviewees may respond with unorganized or rambling answers or move into tangents that are not particularly pertinent to the interview purpose. Sometimes, responses to open questions require a number of follow-up questions. The use of open questions also requires considerable skill by the interviewer. An interviewer who is inexperienced with open-ended questions may find it hard to control the direction of an interview (Stewart & Cash, 1994). Despite these potential difficulties, skillfully asked open-ended questions are very effective for eliciting valuable information that is simply not possible when only relying on closed-ended questions. Open-ended questions open the lines of communication between the interviewee and interviewer in ways that are not possible if closed stimuli are overused.

3. *Use closed questions to elicit specific information, for follow-up, or to focus the interviewee's responses.*

Closed-ended questions are structured to limit interviewees' response options. This type of question is typically used to obtain specific types of information. Closed questions are helpful when interviewers need to check their impressions against those of interviewees (Nirenberg, 1968). There are three basic specificity levels of closed questions. These are:

- Moderately closed questions,
- Highly closed questions, and
- Bipolar questions (Stewart & Cash, 1994).

Moderately closed questions require specific pieces of information from the interviewee. For example, a loan officer might ask the home buyer, "How many bank accounts do you have?" or "How long have you been on your current job?" Such queries anticipate very specific responses, such as having two bank accounts or being on the job for 5 years. **Highly closed questions**, on the other hand, give the interviewee alternatives from which to choose. They must pick from the alternatives offered. For example, a telephone pollster might ask, "Do you watch TV less than 2 hours a day, 2–4 hours a day, 4–6 hours a day, or more than 6 hours a day?" Or, a speech-language pathologist might ask if a client stutters all the time, frequently, occasionally, or almost never. A **bipolar question** is the most highly closed type of question, offering only two response choices. A question might be phrased in such a way that the only responses available are "yes" or "no," that one understands or does not understand, or that the respondent answers "male" or "female." Questions such as whether someone is employed, attends school, or is ready to proceed now with some purchase are examples of bipolar questions.

Closed questions are rather easy for inexperienced interviewers to use. They are easy to control and elicit answers that are short and easy to analyze. A large number of closed questions can be asked in a short period of time, which makes them useful when time is limited. Closed questions are also easy for interviewees to answer because they do not require long explanations (Stewart & Cash, 1994).

However, there are disadvantages to using closed questions. Too many closed questions produce a "question and answer" type of interaction, rather than more of a "give and take" discussion between the parties. Having to respond to a large number of closed questions can also prevent the interviewee from discussing areas of particular interest or importance. The result for the interviewer may be gaining a lot of answers to the questions asked, but not really getting to know the other person and that individual's needs and desires. Too many closed questions can also allow clients to avoid sensitive topics and discourage their discussion and elaboration (Cormier & Hackney, 1987).

4. *Use primary questions to focus a conversation and secondary questions to learn more about the topic of discussion.*

Primary questions introduce a topic of discussion. They are the first questions asked within an area. Primary questions can be open (e.g., "Tell me what brought you in today.") or closed (e.g., "How long has your leg hurt?"). Secondary questions are really follow-up questions. Examples include, "Where exactly does it hurt?" "What does the pain feel like?" "Have you taken anything for the pain?" and "Have you tried to stay off your feet?"

The importance in knowing about these two question types is understanding how they influence the direction and focus of a conversation. Primary questions help introduce a subject area by signaling a new or different direction of a conversation. Secondary questions are used to gain, sometimes one piece at a time, all the information needed within the area introduced by a primary question. Therefore, the primary question must clearly identify the area to be discussed. Secondary questions must be sufficient to fully address all the important factors or issues that would fall under the primary question area.

5. *Understand the difference between neutral and leading questions and how they influence responses.*

Questions in an interview may be either neutral or leading, depending on whether they might influence the interviewee's response or not. Neutral questions allow the interviewee to answer without being unduly influenced by the wording of the question. Leading questions, on the other hand, encourage the interviewee to respond in a specific way. A high school counselor might ask the graduating senior, "Based on our conversation, don't you think XYZ College would be the best school for you?" Or, the hearing aid specialist might ask, "Based on these results, do you see why you would get the most benefit from this hearing aid?" This type of leading question and its inherent bias can make it difficult for respondents to be honest if they really feel differently about the subject. Examples of more neutral questions are, "What colleges seem most appealing to you?" or "Which hearing aid seems to work best for you?"

It is important to understand that bias within a question can occur intentionally or unintentionally. The way a question is asked can influence an interviewee's response. In certain situations, it may be important to ensure that questions are asked neutrally so we do not bias the respondent. Neutral questions can help prevent interviewees from "telling us what we want to hear" rather than what they really feel. In other situations, however, the interviewer might want to lead the respondent with a question. For example, a sales counselor might want to bias a response, such as "Do you see why it is important for you to act now?" Leading questions can cause the respondent to respond in ways that are different from their true feelings; therefore, they should be used carefully.

6. *Understand the various "wh" and "h" questions and the types of information each produces.*

Virtually all journalists have been taught the basic "wh" and "h" questions: who, what, when, where, how, and why. Each question produces different information, whether the questioner is a journalist or any other type of interviewer. Employing these question types allows a structure that many find helpful in interviewing.

Who, what, when, and **where** questions ask for basic facts about a situation (Ivey, 1994). For example, **who** did what, **what** happened, **when** did it occur, **where** did it happen? and so on. The who, what, when, and where questions are useful for obtaining basic facts. Responses to these basic questions become a basis or starting point for the reporter's story. These "wh" questions are also used by the police, teachers, counselors, and professionals in many other areas to obtain basic facts when trying to understand some problem, condition, or situation. However, they fail to address such questions as how and why.

How questions lead to discussion about the sequence of events or the reasoning processes that have led to some situation or someone's feelings about a subject. For example, "**How** did it happen?" may lead to discussion about events leading up to something that happened. A question like, "**How** do you feel about that?" may engender discussion about how someone views a given situation and the events or conditions leading to such feelings. Thus, how questions allow interviewees to explain what preceded some situation and to express their feelings about the situation. How questions, depending on what is asked and wording, can be either leading or neutral. For example, "How did it happen?" is usually a neutral question. But a question like "How could you pass up this offer?" could be very leading. If our goal is simply to obtain some information from the other person, the question should be asked neutrally.

Why questions often lead to a discussion of reasons why something was done—or was not done. The interviewer may ask, "**Why** did you let that happen?" or "**Why** do you think that occurred?" Interviewers need to be careful when asking why questions because they can put the interviewee on the defensive. Such questions may also engender feelings of guilt or be perceived as prying (Dillard & Reilly, 1988).

Another wh-like question is **was**. Asking a was question can put the interviewee on the spot, as in, "**Was** the car traveling too fast"? A good alternative is to be conditional by asking a **could** question. Could questions tend to be nonjudgmental—indicating interviewer tentativeness. "**Could** the car have been traveling too fast?" makes such queries more comfortable to answer. They can also give the person being interviewed some degree of freedom and control of the exchange. If the interviewer asks, "Could you tell me more about that?" the interviewee might feel free to say, "I really don't have any more to add." Such a could question is somewhat open-ended and easy to expand on, but it is also rather easy for the respondent to indicate that there is nothing further to say. Could questions can also suggest some possibility without unduly tieing the interviewee to what is suggested. **Was** requires a full commitment; **could** implies a possibility.

7. Integrate, as appropriate, all the question types into interviewing.

The question types discussed in this chapter—open and closed, primary and secondary, and neutral and leading, as well as the wh questions (who, what, when, where, how, and why, plus could)—do not occur in isolation from each other. For example, a question such as "What brought you in here today?" may be open, primary, and neutral. A question like "Do you want to consider whole-life or term insurance?" is more closed, but it could be primary or secondary, or even neutral or leading, depending on the context. Different combinations can be used during any interview. The important thing is to understand what the goal of asking any particular question is. This then dictates the type of question we might use.

As discussed earlier in the chapter, open questions produce longer responses about a variety of subjects of importance to the interviewee. Closed questions yield shorter answers about specific topics of discussion. Good interviewers use open questions to encourage discussion and discover areas of interest or concern to the party being interviewed. They use closed questions to secure more-specific pieces of information. Often, but not always, the best use of closed questions is as follow-up (secondary) questions to responses from open questions.

In general, an effective interviewer uses a primary question to introduce the area of discussion, then asks the appropriate secondary questions before moving on to the next primary question. This allows both the interviewer and the interviewee to stay on the specific subject until it has been fully discussed. It is generally inappropriate and often confusing to jump from one primary area to another without fully discussing information that should be addressed by follow-up secondary questions.

Realize that every primary question may necessitate a number of follow-up questions, depending on the topic of discussion. It is rare to have a primary question, a single secondary question, another primary question, another secondary question, and so forth. However, there can be a trap in asking too many secondary questions. In instances with time constraints, asking too many secondary questions early in an interview can preclude even addressing some of the other primary questions that should be asked. Therefore, strive for an appropriate balance of primary and secondary questions to cover all the information needed, while not getting "bogged down" within less important areas.

CHAPTER
6

Managing Nonverbal and Verbal Communication

To help ensure success in interviewing, interviewers need to effectively use the various question types discussed in Chapter 5. However, an effective interview involves more than just using questions skillfully. Effective interviews include questions, but there is much more than just asking questions and getting answers. Interviewing is more than a simple conversation; it is a process of purposeful, "give and take" communication between two parties. It also has a specific structure, as described in Chapter 4.

This chapter examines some of the factors and techniques that facilitate or hinder effective communication, including a variety of nonverbal and verbal behaviors. A number of fundamental interviewing techniques and suggestions are also discussed. Also included are several defensive reactions and defense mechanisms that occur during some interactions. The actual treatment of excessive defensiveness or defense mechanisms should be handled by a qualified mental health professional, but, as interviewers deal with people, such behavior will be seen. Some understanding of these reactions and their ramifications is important for everyone who deals with other people.

1. *Use orientations to structure interviews and help focus topics of discussion.*

Orientations are a type of verbal behavior that provide direction or structure to interviews. Authorities on interviewing (Garrett, 1982; Lang, van der Molen, Trower, & Look, 1990; Martin & Hiebert, 1985; Stewart & Cash, 1994) emphasize the importance of beginning an interview with a clear statement of its purpose. They also suggest concluding the interview with a summary of the major points covered and a description of any follow-up activities or next steps that will be needed. These are two fundamental parts of interviews: clear statements of what needs to be done at the beginning and a summary and indication of what will occur next at the end.

Presession orientations, activities before the interview, were described in Chapter 4. Presession orientations are important because they help prepare interviewees for what to expect. Without such orientations, the person being interviewed may have feelings of uncertainty, anxiety, and unnecessary concern going into the interaction. The person who knows what to expect from an encounter will be more likely to open up to the interviewer (Doster, 1972; Shipley, 1992).

Orientations are used during interviews to direct or redirect discussions. These may be in the form of specific **instructions, directions, explanatory statements, summaries**, or **paraphrases**. The interviewer provides instructions and directions to define the subject matter to be discussed. **Instructions** help the person being interviewed understand what is expected; whereas, **directions** tell the interviewee what to talk about next or what actions need to be taken (Ivey, 1994). For example, the interviewer may say, "I need to know about your educational background" or "Describe the symptoms you've been experiencing." Both examples orient interviewees by telling them what to discuss. The interviewer may use an **explanation** to further structure the interview. Explanations describe the reason for some request to interviewees, thereby helping them understand why certain areas need discussion. In essence, explanations help legitimize the needs for certain information.

Brief summaries and paraphrases are used in the body of an interview to clarify topics of discussion. A **paraphrase** "feeds back" some of what the interviewee has said. Paraphrases help convey that we understand about what is being said, or help interviewees understand what they are really conveying.

A **summary** is a recap of what has been learned or covered, also giving the interviewee the chance to add any information necessary or to correct any interviewer misconceptions. Summaries can encourage the person being interviewed to discuss topics in greater detail or signal the need to change topics and "move on" (Mowrer, 1988). For example, the interviewer may say something like, "It sounds like your family feels that _____. They don't seem too comfortable about it. Now I need to know how you feel about _____." In this example, there is a summary of an interviewee's input on how the family feels about the topic, with a change in direction to the interviewee's feelings. A summary can also complete discussion in one area before moving on to a new topic.

When providing information or attempting to influence or persuade someone else, summaries help ensure that whatever information is conveyed is said frequently enough for full understanding. When summarizing, interviewers use their own words to convey their understanding of the interviewee's comments or feelings about a subject. When closing an interview, a more detailed type of summary is used to address all the major topics discussed. A closing summary should highlight the major points discussed, while indicating whether or not the purpose of the interview has been accomplished (Purkey & Schmidt, 1987).

The various orientation techniques are used to give direction to an interaction. They help structure what needs to be discussed and help provide focus to an interview. Rambling interviews that seem to be headed nowhere are often caused by an interviewer not using enough orienting devices—too few instructions, directives, explanatory statements, paraphrases, or summaries.

2. Use encouragers to facilitate responses and elicit information.

The interviewer uses **encouragers** to help interviewees begin to share or to continue talking about topics when further information or clarification is needed (Ivey, 1994; Johnson, 1988; Keane & Verman, 1985; Meier, 1989; Okun, 1992). Encouragers can be single words or phrases such as "fine," "that's interesting," "I see," "yes," or "keep going," or may be vocalizations like "mmm" or "mm-huh." Positive head nods and forward leans can also serve as encouragers.

Studies have shown that the use of encouragers by interviewers increases interviewees' verbalizations, decreases frequency and duration of silent periods, and nurtures positive feelings between interviewees and interviewers (Insko & Cialdini, 1969; Kanfer & McBrearty, 1962; Krumboltz & Thorensen, 1969; Merbaum & Osarchuck, 1975). Encouragers are purposeful behaviors that follow specific comments by interviewers; they are not used randomly. Interviewers need to learn how to use this type of technique, which functions best when used at or near the end of an interviewee's verbalization. For example:

> **Interviewee:** I attended college for 4 years.
> **Interviewer:** I see.
> **Interviewee:** I changed my major three times during those years.
> **Interviewer:** Mm-huh.
> **Interviewee:** I began in education, then changed to physics, and finally decided on engineering.
> **Interviewer:** Keep going.

The person being interviewed is encouraged to keep talking in more detail when interviewers follow specific comments with purposefully used encouragers.

3. Don't use "OK" or "mm-huh" unless you really mean it.

Verbal behaviors such as "OK" and "mm-huh" can serve as encouragers. When used with appropriate vocal tones and at the right times, "OK" and "mm-huh" can communicate "everything is fine," "you are doing well," or "keep talking." This is fine, if this is the interviewer's intention. However, many people use "OK" and "mm-huh" without even knowing it, thereby unintentionally influencing the behavior of others, and not always in desired ways. When used skillfully and inserted at strategic times during interactions, encouragers can be very effective in promoting further discussions. However, some inexperienced and unsophisticated interviewers tend to use "OK" and "mm-huh" unknowingly to fill periods of silence during an interview. When used in such manner, these behaviors may actually disrupt intended communication, make the interviewer appear pretty unsophisticated, or unintentionally reinforce unwanted behaviors in an interviewee. Remember that there is nothing wrong with using "OK," "mmm," or "mm-huh" in interviews, as long as usage is controlled and purposeful. However, the uncontrolled use of these utterances can be detrimental to the interviewer's goals.

4. *Use reflections and clarifications to further clarify and facilitate communication.*

It is important for interviewees to feel that they are being heard and understood. This certainly facilitates effective communication and reflections are useful for this purpose. **Reflections** can be used in much the same way as summaries. An interviewer feeds back the interviewee's very words in a reflection. The three types of reflections used by interviewers are:

- Reflecting the content of the interviewee's message,
- Reflecting both the content and feelings expressed by the interviewee, and
- A short reflection or accentuation of the key words used by the interviewee.

An example of a short reflection, or accentuation, is:

Interviewee: I'll be in big trouble if I do not get the report done tonight.
Interviewer: "Big trouble?"

In this example, we would expect the interviewee to follow up and expand on what is meant by "big trouble." All three types of reflections serve to highlight what the interviewee has conveyed. If phrased somewhat tentatively with a question-like intonation, reflections encourage interviewees to explore a topic further or to correct any possible interviewer misperceptions.

Clarifications are used when some statement made by the interviewee or the interviewee's feelings about a subject need to be more fully understood (Schuyler & Rushmer, 1987). If the interviewee makes a statement that is confusing or unclear, the interviewer tries to clarify the information. The interviewer may say, "Tell me more about the 'bad experience' you had in your previous job." This technique includes phrases such as, "Did I understand you correctly when you said that _____?" When something is not understood, the immediate use of a clarifying comment helps avoid miscommunications and misunderstandings.

5. *Use planned repetitions to ensure understanding.*

Repetition is an important technique, particularly in information-giving and influencing/persuasive/counseling interviews. There are several possible sources of misunderstanding by those being inter-viewed—not understanding the topics of discussion, not under-standing certain terminology or explanations the interviewer uses, interviewee inability to focus on the material because of emotional difficulty, being faced with disturbing or difficult-to-deal-with infor-mation, losing focus because what the interviewer is saying differs from what the interviewee wants to believe, temporary distraction, and others. Even when some of these factors are not present, it can still be difficult for anyone to focus on everything that is said during any interview; few of us can remain fully attentive for prolonged periods of time. It is even more difficult with distractions, whether in the environment or within the mind.

Because the interviewee cannot be expected to maintain full attention at all times, purposefully used repetitions are helpful at key points throughout an interview. It has been said that anything worth saying is worth saying several times. This is certainly true for interviewing, particularly when there is an emotional factor associ-ated with the topics discussed. Whereas repetitions are important and necessary, the wordings of any repetitions should be varied to avoid losing an interviewee's interest or appearing to be conde-scending or disrespectful (Mowrer, 1988).

6. *Use interruptive devices purposefully to redirect conversation.*

In our society, we are taught at an early age that interrupting someone while they are speaking is rude and should be avoided. It has been shown that the more interviewees are interrupted, the less communication takes place (Phillips, Matarazzo, Matarazzo, Saslow, & Kanfer, 1961). However, during certain interviews, it may be nec-essary for the interviewer to use interruptions to change topics and redirect the flow of the interview. This may be needed if the inter-view has moved into topics that are unrelated to the purpose of the interview, if the interviewee is inappropriately "monopolizing" the conversation, or if the discussion has moved into sensitive areas beyond the interviewer's abilities to help (Shipley, 1992).

Interruptions can be used purposefully under certain circum-stances when interviewing excessively verbal people who are talking too much, spending too much time in tangential or unrelated areas, or if interviewees are revealing too much personal information about themselves. An interruption, used carefully, can be a powerful tool to keep an interview on track and at appropriate levels of comfort for both parties. There are various forms of interruptions. A staccato-like, abrupt "uh" may be enough to disrupt the flow of conversation; this is then followed by an indication of what should be discussed next. A more overt interruption involves interjecting something like, "we need to move to _____" or "let's get back to _____." Interruptions must be used carefully as they can be highly disconcerting to the other party. They can be particularly offensive to some individuals from linguistically and culturally diverse cultures, such as the Filipino and Japanese cultures. Too many interruptions, or those which are so abrupt that they irritate the other party, can be very agitating and thereby hamper rapport between the parties.

A more subtle form of interruption has been termed a **guggle** (Richardson, Dohrenwend, & Klein, 1965). Guggles are less offensive, less powerful, but still effective interruptive devices that signal interviewees that some conversational redirection is needed. They serve the same purpose as interruptions, but in a more subtle and potentially less offensive way.

A guggle may be verbal, nonverbal, or vocal. An interviewer might clear the throat or interject a short "ah," "I see," "uh-huh," "that's fine," or other phrase during the interviewee's verbalization. Guggles can be physical movements such as glancing toward a window, checking a watch, shuffling papers, or taking a deep breath. These actions serve to cue the other person that the conversation needs to be changed or terminated.

The examples of verbal guggles just noted ("ah," "I see," "uh-huh," "that's fine") have now been mentioned in two places: earlier in the chapter as encouragers and here as guggles. These are the same verbal or vocal behaviors, the difference being the timing and tone of use. When one of these behaviors is used with an encouraging vocal tone and near the end of an interviewee's comment, it serves to **encourage** continued verbalization. However, the same vocalization or verbalization, if used with a discouraging vocal tone or too early or near the middle of an interviewee's utterance, will serve as a **guggle** and, thereby, inhibit an interviewee's verbalizations. For example, consider the following examples of timing and its effects:

Interviewee: I worked for the company for 5 years and really enjoyed my job.
Interviewer: I see. (An encourager)
Interviewee: I worked for the company for 5 years
Interviewer: I see. (A guggle)

The timing of "I see" in the first example would probably encourage the interviewee to continue talking about the job, the time with the company, or what was enjoyed about the position. However, the timing of the second example might close down further discussion, particularly if the interviewer followed it with a redirection. For example, "I see. I need to know more about _____."

Interruptions and guggles, when utilized, should be done purposefully and consciously. Interviewers need to evaluate their use of verbal, vocal, and nonverbal behaviors to make sure they are not unconsciously using interruptions or guggles during their interactions, as the uncontrolled use of such behaviors adversely hampers interactions. The controlled use of these techniques will encourage appropriate communication within desired areas while keeping both parties on the task at hand.

7. *Be careful with interpretative or evaluative comments.*

Interpretations during an interview go one step beyond what the interviewee has said and attempt to interpret why certain events or feelings may have occurred. In some settings, particularly those dealing with mental health, they are used to provide new perspectives for the interviewee's consideration (Brammer, 1993). Interpretations by interviewers should be used carefully and certainly not inadvertently. There are risks associated with interpreting someone else's words or actions: (a) the untrained person's interpretation can be wrong, (b) being interpreted can cause some interviewees to "clam up," and (c) being interpreted might be remembered by an interviewee long after the interaction is over. Sometimes, interviewees remember little else about the interaction except being interpreted—irrespective of whether the actual interpretation was right or wrong.

When an interpretation is used, the following guidelines are helpful:

- Look for the basic message in the interviewee's comments.
- Provide a paraphrase of what you think the interviewee's message means.
- Convey understanding of the message in terms of your explanation of motives, defenses, and needs.
- Use simple language similar to that used by the interviewee. Avoid wild speculation and technical wordings.
- Indicate that you are giving tentative ideas by prefacing statements such as "The way I see it is _____," "I wonder if is possible that _____," or "Is it possible that _____?"
- Ask for the interviewee's reaction to your interpretation. For example, "Does that seem possible?" (Adapted from Brammer, 1993, p. 95)

Again, interpretations should by used carefully. One's valid interpretation of an interviewee's statement is based on expertise, experience, and insight. Interviewers need to keep in mind that interpretations, irrespective or whether they are correct, can have powerful effects on interviewees. They may inhibit verbalizations and remain an inhibiting factor in future interviews (Kanfer, Phillips, Matarazzo, & Saslow, 1960).

Evaluative comments, those that judge an interviewee's thoughts or actions, should also be used carefully. A number of interviews are conducted to evaluate something or someone, such as job performance interviews. In other interviews, while we may be evaluating something in our minds, we usually have less reason to make evaluative comments. It is important to recognize that evaluative comments are positive or negative judgments about actions, behavior, statements, or feelings. These types of comments often result in decreased conversation from the person evaluated, even if the evaluative comments are positive (Johns, 1975). Interviewees may regard evaluative comments as indications that the interviewer is exhibiting superiority and acting in a judgmental capacity (Powell, 1968). This is particularly true when interviewing someone from another linguistic or cultural background. Again, evaluative comments can be appropriate in some interviewing situations, but may be very inappropriate for others.

8. *Head nods are communicative events to be used purposefully.*

An interviewer can influence communication, positively or negatively, by using certain nonverbal behaviors (Burgoon, 1994; Edinger & Patterson, 1983; Mehrabian, 1972; Shipley, 1992; Siegman & Feldstein, 1987). Head nodding is a specific body movement that indicates either approval or displeasure in the Western culture. Head nodding acts to communicate a message (Dittman, 1987; Thompson, 1973); as such, it has been well-demonstrated that head nodding affects the verbal behavior of interviewees (Fretz, 1966; Mehrabian, 1972; Rosenfeld, 1967).

Positive head nods signal that interviewers are interested in what interviewees are saying, understanding them, or wanting them to keep talking. Positive head nods convey warmth, understanding, and compassion. They tend to encourage an interviewee to continue talking. On the other hand, negative head nods communicate displeasure, disagreement, or disapproval. **Negative head nodding** can make an interviewee insecure about the information being conveyed or even inhibit rapport. Negative nodding tends to discourage communication; interviewees may even change the subject or refrain from further discussion about a topic.

Head nodding, either positive or negative, needs to be controlled during interviews. Nodding is a communicative event that affects interviewees and, subsequently, further discussions. Positive nods should be used purposefully to communicate that we understand or want the other party to continue talking, particularly about the topic being addressed. Negative nods are used to communicate uncertainty, disagreement, or to refocus areas of conversation. Nodding should be done consciously. Many people are unaware that they are nodding; yet they are communicating something with a head nod. They may not, however, be communicating what they are intending!

9. Use body movements and posture to facilitate or inhibit communication.

Body leaning and the posture of people in interview situations is a relatively good indicator of what is happening during the exchange. As with head nods, postural shifts are also communicative events (Scheflen, 1964). The postural change most often noted in interviewing is leaning the body forward or backward. **Forward leans** usually indicate interest, affirmation, or respect. **Backward leans** are signs of disinterest, disagreement, or unfavorable feelings. These can be observed in interviewers or interviewees.

Across most cultures, forward leans can be used purposefully to facilitate communication. An interviewer's forward lean may indicate genuine interest in the interaction or serve to convey warmth or closeness to the other party. Backward leans, conversely, tend to inhibit interviewee verbalization and, consequently, communication (Mehrabian, 1972). As noted in Chapter 2, there are exceptions to this. For example, some individuals from the rural Appalachians may find forward leans unnerving, while a more "belly forward" lean signifies genuine interest (Keefe, 1988).

10. Touch can convey warmth and understanding, or engender concern or distress.

Touching an interviewee can have positive effects on a relationship and the communication that occurs within it, or it can have very damaging effects on a relationship and further communication, depending on how it is done and how the other party perceives it. The most obvious way we often touch others is in a welcoming handshake. Initiating this gesture at the beginning or the end of an interaction is a socially appropriate greeting across most cultures. This can demonstrate an interviewer's warmth when meeting interviewees or indicate satisfaction with an interaction that has occurred. However, depending on how it is done, a handshake can be interpreted in ways that are unintended. For example, a warm and somewhat firm handshake with appropriate distance between the parties can appear "appropriately business-like," although other handshakes, such as having a shorter distance or clasping both hands, can appear more intimate. It should also be noted that some males from certain cultures (e.g., some Middle Eastern cultures) may interpret a handshake from a female as sexually aggressive and expressing potential sexual interest.

Touching in nonintimate, friendly ways during an interview can express warmth and understanding (Kleinke, 1986). This form of touching may help comfort a distressed interviewee, convey support and concern, and it can increase some interviewees' willingness to open up to the interviewer. On the other hand, touching that is inappropriate or perceived as being sexual in nature can impede rapport and even destroy a good working relationship. Such touches are unacceptable and should be avoided. Moursund (1985) provides a useful guideline for interviewers and the use of touch. She says that if there is any question as to the purpose of the touch, a touch should not be used. Individuals react differently to being touched and there are gender and cultural ramifications to touch. One person may perceive a touch as a highly positive, supportive act; another will be distressed. Clearly, touching another person during an interaction is something to consider carefully.

11. *Use eye contact to promote communication, but be aware of its cultural relativity.*

There is general agreement that good eye contact encourages communication (Cormier & Hackney, 1987; Ivey, 1994; Stewart & Cash, 1994). However, the frequency and even the duration of eye contact is culturally relative (Ivey, 1994). In the United States, direct eye contact during communicative exchanges is a characteristic of White, middle-class culture. African Americans tend to use eye contact more when talking and less when listening. In some Hispanic and Asian cultures, it is considered disrespectful for young people to make prolonged eye contact with their elders (Sue, 1988).

In interview situations, the interviewer should maintain direct but gentle eye contact if body language and other indicators signal it facilitates communication. However, eye contact in interviews should not make the other person feel stared at or culturally violated (Shipley, 1992).

12. *Understand the use and effects of pauses and purposeful silences.*

Periods of silence during a conversation are very acceptable within some cultures (e.g., the Arabic culture, Irujo, 1988), but much less acceptable for others. In the general American culture, silence during conversation can be very disconcerting, particularly when the parties are just getting acquainted. For example, one of the bigger fears of many people on a first date is wondering what they will talk about, and if there will be lulls in the conversation. Interviewers are responsible for guiding the direction of an interview; therefore, they are responsible for keeping the conversation going and minimizing any periods of silence. Some inexperienced interviewers, however, make a mistake by trying to break a silence before they really know what to say. It is often much better to say nothing until sure of what direction to take.

There is a type of silence that is very effective in interviewing— specifically, a purposefully used period of silence. Rather than avoiding silent pauses, interviewers can use silence purposefully to influence interactions (Moursund, 1993; Shertzer & Stone, 1980), particularly with clients from backgrounds in which conversational silence is rare or to be avoided. As a technique, silences are periods when interviewers purposefully refrain from commenting, thereby signaling the person being interviewed to respond or to continue speaking (Richardson et al., 1965). A period of silence that is relatively short (e.g., 3 to 5 seconds) and broken by the interviewee tends to increase the length of the interviewee's verbalizations. A longer silence (e.g., 10 to 15 seconds) will most likely be terminated by the interviewer. Longer silences typically result in a shorter verbalization from the person being interviewed (Richardson et al., 1965).

Short periods of silence used purposefully by the interviewer will increase the length of most interviewees' responses for any of the following reasons:

- Interviewees will have time to formulate a response without being interrupted.
- Interviewees will realize that the interviewer wants them to continue or to expand on a previous statement.
- Silence may instill responsibility in the other participant for providing more information or for changing the direction of the interview.

Thus, although the idea of silence in an interview can be somewhat discomforting to many of us, it is actually an important tool. Purposefully used, relatively short periods of withholding comments can increase an interviewee's verbalizations about topics of interest to the interviewer. This is not always possible without the use of such silences.

13. *Probe an area in question to clear up discrepancies.*

Ivey (1994) outlines six types of discrepancies and mixed messages that can occur in interviews. These are:

- **Discrepancies between nonverbal behaviors.** The interviewee may smile and appear relaxed while tightly clenching the fists.
- **Discrepancies between two or more statements.** "I'd really like to get a job, but I'm enjoying my time off."
- **Discrepancies between what one says and what one does.** The interviewee agrees wholeheartedly that regular exercise will improve the individual's condition, but spends evenings reading the paper and watching TV.
- **Discrepancy between a statement and nonverbal behavior.** The parent says that a son's poor grades are of no concern; meanwhile, tears swell in the parent's eyes.
- **Discrepancy between different people.** A husband and wife disagree about the impact of unemployment on their lives.
- **Discrepancies between a client and a situation.** (Adapted from Ivey, 1994, pp. 79–80)

When an interviewer identifies an important discrepancy, it can often be cleared up rather easily by probing the area in question. The interviewer may say something like, "Let's see if I've got this straight, you said, _____." Other times, the interviewer may have to identify the discrepancy for the party being interviewed. In this case, a more direct approach is necessary, such as "Mr. Smith, you said that being out of work doesn't bother you, but how you said it might suggest otherwise. How do you really feel about not having a job?" Most discrepancies and mixed messages can be cleared up or understood better when the interviewer approaches the discrepancy in a direct but nonthreatening manner.

14. *Use confrontation carefully and purposefully.*

Confrontation is a powerful technique used to help interviewees move toward some action or commitment or to deal with realities that they may be avoiding or denying (Brammer, 1993; Cormier &

Hackney, 1987; Kennedy, 1977). A **confrontation** can be useful when helping someone realize that their goals and actions differ or to explore other types of discrepancies. The word confrontation might be taken to mean something mean-spirited or hostile, but this is not what is meant by interview confrontation and certainly not the way it is used in these interactions. Rather, interview confrontations are used without malice or ill feelings. They are tools to directly address some area. Because confrontations are so powerful, they should be used purposefully and carefully.

One example of a confrontation is a "you said _____, but _____" format. For example, "You said you wanted help, but you've missed your last two appointments" or "You said you did your homework, but you haven't turned it in." If possible, the interviewee should not feel trapped by a confrontation, but feel that their best interests are being considered. To accomplish this, interviewers typically need to use a very accepting tone of voice for any confrontation (Lang et al., 1990). Confrontations, when used appropriately, can promote necessary understanding of a situation or actions. Confrontational techniques should be used with consideration of the other person— not as criticism or nagging. Some care is also necessary when using confrontations across cultures; they can be highly disconcerting to some individuals from backgrounds in which indirectness is a prized value.

15. *Resistance should be recognized and, if necessary, dealt with directly.*

Resistance in an interviewee may occur for many reasons, including fears of change or of a new situation (Okun, 1992; Orr & Adams, 1987). An interviewee might demonstrate resistance by lateness, "forgetting" appointments, changing topics of conversation abruptly, being inattentive, being silent or minimally communicative, or failing to follow suggestions made by the interviewer.

Resistance can surface if the interviewee disagrees with the opinions of the interviewer. The interviewee who develops bad feelings toward the interviewer may display resistance. If this is the case, the interviewer should try to develop a better working relationship with the interviewee. Often the resistance can be overcome in time with the development of trust and a more solid relationship. In more extreme cases, a form of confrontation may be needed. The client's resistive behavior is addressed directly to open discussion about what is behind the resistance. For example, "You are coming here for help, but are not talking with me" or "You say you want to get better, but are not going to your physical therapy."

16. *Recognize the presence of denial.*

Denial may be present when a person fails to recognize a problem, fails to see the magnitude of some difficulties, or rationalizes or minimizes certain actions. Interviewees with a problem who are not ready to acknowledge the presence of a difficulty may need time, support and, if appropriate, confrontation to help them see or begin to deal with the problem and its reality. When conducted with care and empathy, conversation that includes confrontation can help many interviewees face a problem situation and begin to remedy it. Without skill, care, and empathy, however, the opportunities to help may be severely damaged. Of course, dealing with more severe or persistent forms of denial falls within the realm of a mental health professional. Denial as a defense mechanism is addressed further a little later in this chapter (see p. 80).

17. *Be aware of information gaps, but be careful not to overinfer anything from them.*

An information gap is defined as some break, or void, in information. For example, when asking someone about their personal history, there may be periods of time in which there is only faint recollection or even no recollection about events at a given time. In some psychological work, certain information gaps are considered potentially significant, as specific information may have been repressed. However, in most interviewing situations, other factors may be present, including: the amount of time between the event in question and the interview, other events that occurred at the same time, or medical-, memory-, or trauma-related problems at that time. These are just a few of the factors that may create gaps in knowledge.

The interviewer may need to consider carefully why an information gap is occurring, but should not necessarily assume that the person is "hiding information" or suffering from an emotionally related blockage. In some cases, if the information sought is truly important, it may need to be obtained from family members or other persons who are familiar with the individual. If an individual is suspected of withholding certain information, time and patience may be needed or the person may need to be convinced that the information is necessary. Different forms of confrontation may be necessary in some of these situations.

18. *Deal directly with recurrent themes.*

A recurrent theme is a topic that a person returns to on several occasions during interactions. Examples of recurrent themes could include such topics as the costs of a particular product or service, what caused a particular problem, whether some situation will turn out well, or many others. Basically, anything of concern to an individual can be a recurrent theme.

Working with recurrent themes can be positive, because the topics of major concern are very identifiable; this is certainly preferable to the other party having something of concern that is never stated. In many cases, interviewers must deal with a recurrent theme at some point to be fully successful. If the interviewee's concern is not addressed, it often continues to reappear until the concerns have been resolved—or until the interviewee decides that the interviewer is not interested or concerned, does not understand, is unconcerned, or cannot handle the question or concern. Failure to address recurrent themes may result in considerable frustration or resistance from interviewees. In some settings, the person may simply end up seeking services elsewhere.

Recurrent themes should be dealt with directly and immediately. One reason to resolve these issues as soon as possible is to allow the interviewee to concentrate on other important areas. For instance, if an interviewee is very concerned about a child's school grades, the parent may have considerable difficulty focusing on the teacher's evaluation of the child's behavior until the concern about grades is addressed. Or, someone may hear very little about the overall benefits of some product or service until the question of costs is addressed.

The interviewer judges how to deal with recurrent themes based on how frequently they occur, their content, and the degree of concern being expressed. If the recurrent theme focuses on past actions or events, the interviewer may use these as a basis for discussing the present or the future. If the interviewee displays deep-seated feelings of guilt, referral to a mental health professional may be necessary. In addressing recurrent themes, the interviewer should be careful to keep the interview on track and not accidentally reinforce unproductive recurrent themes that have previously been dealt with, or problems for which there is no real solution.

19. *Recognize the effects of emotions on communication.*

Emotional states act on both interviewers and interviewees. How individuals feel, in general, about events going on in their lives or, specifically, about topics being discussed, can affect them during interviews. Professionals conducting interviews need to be responsible for not allowing their own emotional states to influence communication during interviews. In most cases, the interviewer is there to meet the client's needs first. The interviewer needs to understand and recognize the effects of emotional states and feelings on the communication that takes place during interviews.

Sometimes how interviewees are feeling is apparent or even expressed; other times it is not. Some of the more common emotions experienced in interviewing situations are **disappointment**, **guilt**, **anger**, and **anxiousness**. **Disappointment** is a natural reaction to a situation that does not correspond with someone's anticipations. People become disappointed when something anticipated or hoped for does not occur. Interviewees may be disappointed when they are not offered the job they want, if they are not approved for the entire loan requested, when the physician's diagnosis is worse than expected, and so forth. Feelings of disappointment are natural reactions to be recognized and understood. The interviewer may need to express empathy and help the interviewee accept the reality of the situation.

Feelings of **guilt** can occur when someone feels ashamed about some feelings or actions, past or present, or their role in some situation. People may feel that they created a problem because of something they did, because they failed to do something sooner, or because they did something that now appears to be wrong (Hartbauer, 1978). Feelings of guilt may be evident in an initial interview, but such feelings may not emerge until an interviewee feels more comfortable with the interviewer over time or even starts to learn more about some subject. In other words, expression of guilt may or may not emerge early within a relationship.

Certain topics can engender feelings of guilt. As examples, a physician might ask parents why they did not have their ill child seen earlier or a credit counselor might ask why someone continued to charge new purchases while current bills were not being paid. Under some circumstances, interviewees may get the impression that the interviewer is blaming them for some situation, rather than being sympathetic or understanding. Interviewers in this situation may need to reassure the interviewee to counter feelings of guilt. Often, several reassurances are necessary but even multiple reassurances may not resolve more deep-seated feelings of guilt immediately. The interviewer should remain objective, listen to the feelings of interviewees and, if appropriate, try to correct any misunderstandings or misperceptions they may have. Typically, the interviewer should not provide false assurances to assuage guilty feelings. It is usually inappropriate to convey that someone did not do something wrong—if indeed they did. However, the interviewer's efforts are better spent focusing on what can be done in the future, and in helping the interviewee move from counterproductive guilt feelings to constructive present and future feelings and actions.

People's thresholds of **anger** and how they handle that anger differ considerably. Some people seem to "blow up" with little apparent provocation; others seem to "take things in stride." Some individuals show their anger quickly; with others anger seems to fester inside. The expression of anger is also culturally related. For example, the expression of anger would be inappropriate in many interview situations by some members of certain Asian cultures, but that does not mean that anger is not being felt by the individual. The emotion of anger may be related to frustration, feeling threatened, or negative feelings about oneself or others (Hackney & Cormier, 1994). Expressions of anger during an interview can occur for a number of reasons. Some interviewees may not like the interviewer, not understand why they are being interviewed, disagree with what is being said or asked, or be unhappy about being unable to resolve some problem themselves. Anger may also be related to how an individual has learned to "solve" situations, to immaturity, or whatever.

When anger is directed at the person conducting an interview, the interviewer should first evaluate any aspects of their own behavior that could be contributing to the anger. The interviewer may have been late for the interview, used technical terminology that the interviewee did not understand, did not understand what the interviewee was really saying, accidentally implied something that was not meant, contradicted an important cultural value, or any of numerous other reasons. Other times, however, the interviewer may simply be the most available person to receive the brunt of an interviewee's anger.

It should also be noted that the expression of anger can be a positive step or event, particularly within the mental health professions. For example, the expression of anger in psychotherapeutic work may signal that an individual is beginning to recognize and deal with certain feelings or events. There is no magical way for most interviewers to deal with all feelings of anger. In general, the best way to deal with interviewees' anger is to allow them to vent their feelings while listening carefully. Often, an angry person just needs someone to listen while expressing and releasing the anger. Once the anger has been voiced and the emotion released, more desirable forms of communication can resume or begin.

Some degree of **anxiety** is a somewhat normal aspect of many interview situations, as discussed in the section on apprehension in Chapter 1. It is somewhat normal for both the person doing the interviewing and the person being interviewed to have some apprehensions about the situation. However, excessive anxiety within interview situations is counterproductive and hampers the communication that should be occurring during these interactions. Sources of anxiety for the interviewee can range from the interviewer's personality or methods or attitudes, to questions about what will result from the interview or doubts about the interviewer's abilities (Hartbauer, 1978). Interviewing across cultures can also lead to anxiety, particularly when one or both parties are insecure or lack cultural awareness and sensitivity.

Anxiety is usually pretty easy to detect within the context of what interviewees say and how they say it, as well as in such nonverbal behaviors as fidgeting, averting eye contact, changing body positions, and so forth. It may also be manifested in the respondent not really answering certain questions or giving very guarded or cursory responses to questions. The interviewee with excessive anxiety may be hesitant, passive, angry, or even verbally aggressive. It is often a good idea to encourage the expression of anxiety. Once expressed, the interviewer can provide the person being interviewed with more objective information and, if appropriate, reassurance that the interviewer cares and wants to help.

20. *Recognize defensive reactions and defense mechanisms.*

Physical and emotional self-protection is a basic human instinct. Defending ourself or a loved one is certainly very normal, but problems emerge from excessive, unnecessary, or inappropriate defensiveness. Defensiveness can be observed in some people as they seek to maintain self-esteem while "buying time" to begin resolving some problem. However, defensive behavior can be a problem in interviews, because it interferes with good, open communication and appropriate follow-up actions that should be taken. Defensive feelings can develop from a variety of sources. Some of the more common sources include interviewees feeling misunderstood or picked on, or when they become frustrated by opinions or values that conflict with their own.

Sigmund Freud was the pioneer of modern psychoanalysis and his thoughts about a variety of topics have spawned considerable progress within the helping professions. Freud's thoughts about defense mechanisms are now part of established mental health parlance. Because defensiveness and defense mechanisms are frequently encountered in interview situations, several basic defense mechanisms are described here briefly. In reading the following material, remember that some degree of defending oneself is absolutely normal. Excessive defensiveness, however, becomes a concern in interviews when it hinders progress or disrupts communication.

A typical defensive reaction is **denial**, in which some reality or personal problem is avoided by denying that the situation, condition, or problem exists. What may be very apparent to everyone else is denied by the individual in question. Serious forms of psychological denial, for example, are often encountered by professionals working in the field of chemical dependence. It is very common, when talking with a seriously involved practicing alcoholic or drug addict, to hear that person vehemently deny that there is any problem or that chemical use is harming the person's life, or the lives of others. This is denial.

A form of denial sometimes encountered is **minimization**. The existence or severity of a given situation is minimized—or made out to be less than it really is. Again, in the field of chemical dependence minimization is encountered frequently. For example, when asking a practicing alcoholic how much alcohol is being consumed, it is very common for that person to report considerably less than is actually being consumed. The same person might also argue that the addiction has had little effect on the family, job, or friends. This person is minimizing the problem and its effects.

Rationalization involves a logical but untrue explanation of some undesirable behavior. Rationalizations allow the individual to explain why some expectations have not materialized. In effect, rationalizing allows us to justify our actions or failures. Not getting something done because we were too busy, doing poorly in a class because the teacher doesn't like us, not being promoted because of favoritism toward another worker, or drinking too much because a spouse is difficult to live with, are examples of rationalizations. If the contention were true, then it might be a legitimate concern or complaint. However, in many cases, it is a defense mechanism being used to protect one's self-esteem rather than deal with some reality. Interviewers sometimes encounter rationalizations as a form of resistance. The person to be interviewed may make excuses for not being at an interview or, if present, for not sharing certain information or failing to follow-up on something that had been recommended.

Projection is seeing in others what is actually a shortcoming or problem within one's self. Interviewees may use projection, which distorts reality by attempting to relocate the blame for personal failures or frustrations onto someone else. Thus, responsibility for something, often a failure, is shifted from oneself to another person. Anyone can be the target of projection. A parent might be criticized for not listening to a teenager when, in fact, the adolescent refuses to listen to the parent. A nursing home operator might be wrongly accused of being insensitive to an elderly patient by someone who has never even visited that person. Interviewers are frequently the targets of projections, particularly when sadness or misfortune are involved (Hutchinson, 1979; Schum, 1986). The interviewer must realize that those who are projecting are trying to satisfy their needs for ego protection.

Displacement is a transference of hostile feelings from the responsible person or problem to a "safe" person or object. Displacement results in "kicking the dog" or "taking it out on the one you love" types of actions. A frequently cited example of displacement is slamming a door when someone is really mad at someone or something else, not the door. In an interview situation, the person conducting the interview may become the safe person upon whom to take out aggression. The immediate needs for the interviewee to vent anger is satisfied by "dumping" on the interviewer. Displacement can cause irritation, hurt feelings, and severe disruptions of communication between parties. Because displacement occurs, it is important for interviewers to realize what is happening. It may not be the interviewer who is really the source of the problem. If the interviewer reacts angrily, important opportunities for effective communication may be lost.

Suppression is a defensive reaction in which individuals control their impulses, wishes, and desires. Their true feelings are kept inside and may even be denied publicly. This defense mechanism can be counterproductive in interviews, because it limits true communication. One step beyond suppression is **repression** (Clarke, 1968). Instead of just controlling feelings, the individual exhibiting repression actually blocks out the feelings to the point that they are not recognized by the person. This individual is truly unaware or unconscious that a problem exists. Repression can be exasperating for interviewers, particularly when dealing with serious problems. Full communication between the interviewer and interviewee cannot occur if the interviewee has repressed true feelings about the situation.

Reaction formations are more unusual, and they can be difficult to detect by those outside of the mental health professions. In a reaction formation, the individual has actually developed thoughts and attitudes that are very different from how the individual truly feels deep inside. There is, in a sense, so strong a denial that new thoughts actually replace the older, unacceptable feelings. Reaction formation can be illustrated by an individual who has become convinced that, against all odds, their loved one will be the one in a million who overcomes some difficulty. We are by no means suggesting that hope is an unimportant quality, but the reality is truly distorted for someone suffering from reaction formation. An important thing to realize is that, like some other defense mechanisms, reaction formation occurs at a subconscious level; the patient is not aware of the feelings being covered up. Hutchinson (1979) points out that this particular defense mechanism is difficult for untrained persons to deal with; referral for psychotherapy is typically necessary with this mechanism.

In concluding this section, readers need to be aware that there are a number of types of defensive reactions and defense mechanisms that can occur within interactions. These must be dealt with in some settings, but not in others. The recognition of such reactions and patterns is critical for those in fields that must work with such problems, such as mental health. Recognition, however, is also important for those in many other fields because it helps us begin to understand some of the patterns and behaviors being encountered. Such recognition also helps identify when a referral may be indicated, if appropriate. Information about making a referral is in Chapter 7 (pp. 94–95).

CHAPTER
7

Various Thoughts, Suggestions, and Concluding Matters

The skillful use of interviewing techniques is an important factor in the success of an interview. Also needed is a solid knowledge of the given field, as well as the abilities to adequately obtain and convey information to achieve the results desired. These factors, combined with caring attitudes and professionalism, contribute to success in interviewing.

Professionalism involves being fully qualified and having ethical integrity (Drapela, 1983; Orr & Adams, 1987). Part of professionalism is knowing our boundaries and limits and being cautious about overstepping these boundaries. Often, the overall success of an interview is related to the professionalism and skill levels of the interviewer. In the following sections, a number of factors that relate to professionalism, dealing with different situations that emerge in some interviews, and interviewer development are discussed.

1. *Be aware of personal biases, beliefs, and attitudes that can affect interactions.*

Every interviewer has personal beliefs and even prejudices about certain topics or matters. Becoming a good interviewer involves recognizing personal biases and stereotypes so as not to be inadvertently or inappropriately influenced by them. Several basic tools of good interviewers include having empathy, exercising good judgment, and being fair-minded.

In addition to personal biases or beliefs, interviewers can also carry personal issues with them into interviews. A listing of personal issues could be very long—certain fears, notions of how other people should respond to certain situations, and many more. Depending on the situation, personal issues may be extremely inappropriate to take into an interaction. The first step toward not carrying these into interviews is simply to recognize their existence as personal beliefs or issues. Until so recognized, there is no basis for understanding their possible influence during certain interviews.

2. *Do not discriminate.*

Discrimination on the basis of age, cultural heritage, disability, gender, race, religion, or sexual orientation is inappropriate at any time. Professional interviewers are aware that discrimination is inappropriate and, depending on the work environment, often illegal. It is incumbent on professional interviewers to provide appropriate, nondiscriminatory service to all who interact with them. Part of avoiding discrimination is being culturally aware and sensitive.

3. *Stay within your own levels of abilities and training.*

Interviewers should recognize their own areas of expertise and levels of training and not go beyond these. One should not attempt to use techniques or approaches, or move into areas of knowledge and authority, that are the province of other professionals (e.g., a family practice physician should not attempt psychoanalysis, a nonphysician should not attempt a medical diagnosis, an attorney specializing in criminal law should not provide counsel in patent law, etc.). Moving into areas that are beyond one's scope of expertise runs real risks of being unsuccessful and even can be dangerous. When dealing with people, as Black (1982) has commented, shun the role of being an amateur psychologist.

4. *Represent yourself honestly.*

Interviewees should be able to look around an interviewer's room and get a pretty good feel for the interviewer—who the person is and what the person does. There may be certain books on the bookshelf, diplomas or pictures on the wall, or items on a desk that help represent who the interviewer is, the person's personality, or interests. The setting should represent the individuals who work there—not who or what they are not. Likewise, interviewers should never verbally profess to be something they are not or make any claims that are untrue.

5. *Don't allow technique to be a substitute for caring.*

We have discussed skillful use of various interviewing techniques. Such techniques are used to help achieve purposes skillfully and efficiently, but these tools are not a substitute for caring attitudes or common sense. For example, if a question asked evokes painful memories and an emotional response from the person being interviewed, natural tendencies to comfort and reassure the interviewee may be needed. Interviewers should not have to refer to a book to deal with a situation that is happening.

In most settings, interviewers should avoid "being clever" or "tricking" the other party to get information or secure agreement. If an interviewee's responses seem vague or there appear to be discrepancies, the interviewer can ask direct questions to help uncover the information needed. The interviewer can point out discrepancies, but certainly not in a "Ha! I caught you." manner. The interviewer's responsibility is to discover or to present information; only a few interviewing roles (e.g., a detective or attorney under certain conditions) involve obtaining information or agreement in "more clever" fashions.

6. *Understand the role of advice.*

Probably one of the earth's most plentiful resources is advice. Unfortunately, much advice given is unsolicited and, many times, based on very little other than someone else's concept of what is real, true, or a good or bad idea. Almost everyone realizes that advice can be good, bad, or somewhere in between. Interviewers who offer advice within their discipline or occupation base their suggestions on knowledge of their field and the other party's needs and circumstances. This is the true difference between professionally based advice and advice that is outside of our areas of expertise. Our job, as interviewers, is to limit ourselves to those areas of personal and professional expertise.

7. *When unsure of something said, seek clarification.*

In Chapter 1, we noted some of the apprehensions and fears that are part of interviewing situations. Because of these apprehensions and the nature of human communication, misunderstandings can occur rather easily in interviews. For example, interviewees who are talking about a personal history (medical, educational, financial, or other) may be simultaneously trying to reconstruct the past, collect their thoughts, formulate intelligent responses, appear knowledgeable, and please the interviewer. It is possible for thoughts to get jumbled or out of sequence or for responses to be incomplete. An interviewer's job may be to help clarify these responses, while preventing or at least minimizing the possibility of misunderstandings. If an interviewee's response is unclear, the interviewer can ask a direct question or use techniques such as a summary or paraphrase for clarification. For example, "Do I understand that _____?" or "What I hear you saying is _____." Immediately clarifying information helps keep misunderstandings to a minimum.

When conveying information, it is important to keep language understandable and repeat any key points being made. Of course, the wording needs to vary when repeating key pieces of information and interviewers need to continually look for signs that the other person is confused or not understanding what has been said.

8. *When unsure about some information, say so. Then find out and get back to the interviewee.*

Imagine asking a physician some question of great personal concern. If the doctor did not know the answer, we would hope that individual would check reference materials, contact other specialists, or do both to get the correct answer. How would we feel if the physician did not know the correct answer, was ashamed to admit this, gave us some incorrect answer to satisfy our concerns, and then sent us on our way? Clearly, this would be very unprofessional and inappropriate. Depending on the nature of the condition, such an approach could have some very serious negative consequences. The same principle holds true for interviewing in many occupations; interviewers should not try to "bluff" something when they do not know the correct answer. Incorrect information can have serious negative consequences in most fields. Also, from a practical standpoint, truth has a way of emerging across time, causing a loss of credibility for those who are dishonest. When faced with not knowing the answer to a particular question, honest interviewers who are acting responsibly are not afraid to admit that they do not know the answer, but find out what is needed and let the other party know. For example, it is appropriate to say something like, "I don't know, but I will find out and get back to you."

9. *When in doubt about what to say, consider saying nothing.*

There are times in human communication when something happens or someone says something and we truly have no response that seems appropriate. This can happen, for example, if someone says something so outlandish or inappropriate that we are simply unable to respond in a suitable fashion. Another example may be seen in grief, when we simply do not know what to say to help comfort a person experiencing a deep loss. When unsure of quite what to say, it is often best to say nothing. Attempts to "bumble our way" through such moments often come off very poorly or inappropriately. In the case of grief, it may be appropriate simply to demonstrate our silent, concerned support. Sometimes the most effective form of support is just being there, listening and, if appropriate, perhaps providing a caring touch to indicate that we are there and care.

10. *Understand the differences between accepting and condoning.*

It is possible to accept a situation or a person's action without condoning it. There is a sign that states, "Smokers are loved and welcomed here, smoking is not." The idea behind the sign is that the person is loved and accepted. That the person smokes is accepted. However, the activity of smoking is not accepted. In this case, there are at least two levels of acceptance and one level of nonacceptance.

Now let's consider a family's acceptance and condoning of smoking. If someone in the family smokes, the whole family probably **accepts** that this occurs. However, this does not mean that they approve of or **condone** the smoking. They would rather that their loved one did not smoke in most cases. This family accepts the reality of smoking occurring, but does not condone it.

Certain interview situations may require us to accept something, but not condone it. For example, in an abuse situation, we may accept that someone was very angry but it is inappropriate to condone any abuse that resulted. In this case, a verbalization like "You sound like you were very angry" might be appropriate, but saying "I can understand why you struck out" would be inappropriate. The same principle holds true in certain sales situations— one may accept that a person is not going to buy some product but may not condone the reasons for failing to make the purchase. What is sometimes helpful to remember is that acceptance of the other person, and aspects of their behavior, is needed. But, this does not necessarily mean having to condone inappropriate types of behavior. Like the sign about smoking, interviewers may need to be precise about what is acceptable, not acceptable, condoned, or not condoned.

11. *Realize that agreement does not mean empathy.*

The terms agreement and empathy have different meanings (Meier & Davis, 1993). **Agreement** means that two parties are in assent about something. **Empathy**, on the other hand, involves a sharing of feelings or spirit. As an interviewer, one may agree with what the interviewee is saying without understanding their true feelings and emotions. For example, the interviewer hearing an interviewee's account of a serious automobile accident will agree that the accident was traumatic. Agreeing with the interviewee's experience, however, does not mean that the interviewer fully understands the traumas and emotions felt by the interviewee. The more empathetic interviewers are, the greater their abilities to actually feel and share the emotions and feelings of another person. Interviewers should evaluate their abilities to empathize with interviewees, as this can add powerful insight into what others are thinking and feeling. Interviewees generally appreciate an interviewer who can truly be empathetic with them.

12. *Realize the differences between reliability and validity.*

Reliability and validity are vital factors in scientific research and, indeed, in interacting with other people. These two factors should be evaluated carefully in interviewing. **Reliability** represents consistency. The reliability of information from an information-getting interview may be determined by the consistency of the information across different meetings with the same individual, across different individuals, or by comparing information from an interview with other types of information received over time. In effect, is the information given consistent or does it vary? The **validity** of information is based on whether the information is actually true.

Interviewers need to realize that reliability and validity are both important, but distinctly different. Information given by an interviewee may be reliable (i.e., consistent), but not valid (i.e., accurate or true). For example, someone who is telling us what we want to hear may be very consistent in these expressions, but the information may be very different from how the person actually feels. On the other hand, someone may be sharing information that is fundamentally valid, but has inconsistencies within it. Depending on the setting and type of work involved, both reliability and validity need to be assessed carefully by interviewers.

13. *Understand the difference between a fact and someone's interpretation of a fact.*

There is a game in which a picture is shown to the first player at one end of a room. Player 1 looks at the picture for a few seconds, draws an interpretation of the picture, then passes the drawing just made to Player 2. The second player draws an interpretation of the picture and shows it to Player 3, who then draws the picture. This continues, one person at a time, through everyone in the room. When the final original drawing is made, it is compared to the original picture. Usually the last picture drawn is considerably different than the original. A variation of this game is to whisper a secret, one person at a time, around a room. The message that ends up is usually very different than the first message shared. Both activities can be used as object lessons in how something changes as it is passed across people. The moral of these examples can also be applied to interviewing, particularly as we view information transferred across people. Interviewers will encounter people whose knowledge is "first hand" and others whose information was passed down through others. Reliability and validity problems can occur in either situation, and both generally become more problematic across time and as more people become involved.

There is also the issue of a fact versus someone's interpretation of a fact. For example, that two cars collided is probably an observable fact. However, interpretations about that fact can differ considerably. One person might say that car A hit car B; another person might report that car B hit car A. Interpretations of "why" it happened by either or both parties might range from speeding to not signalling, falling asleep at the wheel, intoxication, and so on. It is not very unusual for at least one party, and sometimes both parties, to be inaccurate in their interpretations. However, this does not change the basic fact that two cars collided and, in all likelihood, at least one party is probably responsible.

The interviewer may need to assess what is true and what someone believes to be true. Consciously considering fact—versus someone's interpretations of fact—can help interviewers begin to separate out their thinking within these areas.

14. *If needed, check representations of fact against your own observations and data available.*

There is little need to check information obtained in many interview situations. However, if appropriate to a given setting, the validity of interviewee's information can be checked in several different ways. Some basic questions interviewers can ask themselves include:

- Can the information be verified or reproduced?
- Is adequate and reliable verifying information available?
- Is the information coming from one or several sources?
- Does information obtained from tests, records, and background information correspond with information obtained orally?
- Does the information correspond with professional judgment and the knowledgeable opinions of others?
- Does the interviewee provide information without reluctance or hesitation? (Shipley, 1992)

Basic information will need to be confirmed in some settings. For example, many employers insist on taking a job application, obtaining references, having applicants take some form of a performance or knowledge test, as well as undergoing an interview. Interviewers in these settings should not be mistrustful of all interviewees, but they still need to check for validity and reliability, as some percentage of respondents will not be fully honest with them.

15. *Avoid jumping to premature conclusions.*

The old adage, "You can't judge a book by its cover," is applicable to interviewing. Because someone is 7 feet tall does not mean the person plays or even likes basketball. The nervous person who cannot look you in the eye may be telling the truth, while the calm, honest-looking person may be looking you straight in the eyes while lying. Judgments should be made very cautiously on the basis of appearance, second-hand information, or partial information. The interviewer should remain objective and open to give those being interviewed a fair chance without jumping to premature conclusions.

16. *Be candid but kind when conveying "bad news," when culturally appropriate.*

Being the bearer of bad news is never easy. However, there are appropriate and inappropriate ways of providing bad news. The most appropriate manner in the general American culture is being blunt but kind; whereas not being candid or sensitive is considered inappropriate in delivering bad news. A young Anglo couple awaiting news about a home loan does not want a loan officer to "tip-toe" toward the bank's conclusion, nor are they interested in hearing a long description of bank policies before being turned down. But, neither do they want to be told, "Sorry, but your credit stinks." The loan officer could handle this situation more appropriately by saying, "Due to your credit rating at this time, the bank is unable to approve your application. Although this is disappointing, I'd like to show you some ways to improve your credit." Bad news should be delivered directly and with kindness. When possible, it is helpful to offer recipients of bad news something constructive to do to feel useful and productive. It can be very frustrating to receive bad news without anything constructive to do or at least consider.

Being candid can be difficult, but it is a responsibility that should be shouldered directly. Being evasive, "beating around the bush," or withholding important information is generally inappropriate—and often just postpones the inevitable need to face some situation directly. Many times, postponing the inevitable also makes it even more difficult to do later.

There is some cultural variability that applies to providing bad news. For example, speaking less directly than described earlier is considered more appropriate within the Arabic culture. In other cultures, such as the Native American culture, bad news is also conveyed less directly, or at least preceded by more positive things about the person or situation (Gilliland, 1992).

17. *Understand that hostility can be generated by the interviewer, or by circumstances outside of the interviewer.*

There are many possible reasons why interviewees can be hostile, including circumstances created by something completely independent of the interview situation. Or, hostility may be related to the setting, what has occurred within the interview, something that was said, something that was not said, or many other factors. The interviewer, of course, may be the cause of the hostility. When dealing with people, and their feelings and beliefs, it is possible to inadvertently offend someone. Perhaps the interviewer made an insensitive comment, pushed some point too hard, missed the point of what the other person said, kept the person waiting too long, appeared distracted, or did something else that offended or irritated the interviewee.

An interviewee's hostility can also stem from something that happened earlier in the same setting, a previous interaction with an insensitive professional, fear, or some other frustration (Shipley, 1992). In a few cases, hostility can simply result from having a bad morning. The interviewee may have been rushed and unable to start the day with a normal routine, gotten stuck in traffic, received a traffic ticket, or had difficulty finding a parking place. Such a person might just need a few minutes to calm down and vent some frustration before real communication can take place.

The point is to understand that there are many possible sources of hostility. Interviewers may need to judge the real sources of frustration to proceed appropriately and constructively. If an event triggering hostility is outside of the interviewer's control and purview, it may be helpful to let the person vent some of the frustrations while listening attentively. If, on the other hand, there is something the interviewer is doing to create hostility, this needs to be recognized, because it will be the basis for modifying the interaction with the other person.

When helping people vent or release anger, interviewers may need to be "emotional lighting rods" to allow for constructive venting. A clarifying probe may help reveal a source of anger and allow the interviewee to release the hostility. The interviewer might say something like, "Something seems to be bothering you." "You seem a little angry at _____," or "I sense you're upset with _____." When encountering hostility, interviewers must remain in control of themselves, rather than also getting angry. One party with anger or hostility can be tough enough; having two angry or hostile parties can be a true mess.

While giving the interviewee the chance to ventilate, interviewers should monitor the timing of anything said to the interviewee. When interviewers respond too quickly during an interviewee's ventilations, the interviewer can appear superficial or defensive, which can further fuel the interviewee's feelings of hostility. Interviewers should allow an interviewee to express the full range of feelings without being interrupted. The interviewer can also feed back the feelings expressed by the interviewee. For example, "It does sound frustrating to _____." Letting interviewees know that you understand their feelings can help reduce their hostility, while letting them know that you care and are hearing them.

It can be tempting for some interviewers to ignore hostile feelings, rather than deal with them openly and directly. This rarely solves anything and often results in noncommunicative interactions and frustration for both parties. Again, hostile feelings typically need to be dealt with before optimal communication can occur.

18. *Avoid criticizing other people.*

When interviewees come to us, they may have already sought the advice or counsel of several people, perhaps even several different professionals. It is possible that they have already received varied and even conflicting information. If asked about these different opinions, most professional interviewers are careful to avoid criticizing other people, even when they know the other information is incorrect or inappropriate. Criticism of others has a way of making us look bad even when we are right. Thus, we need to "walk a higher plane."

One way of avoiding criticism of others is to limit our discussions to what we know, our own direct observations or testing, and any other bases of first-hand knowledge. It is sometimes helpful if the other person understands that what we are finding or suggesting is based on our observations at the point in time. It is possible that what someone else observed or suggested at a different time was true then, but our concern is the present. Remember that criticizing other professionals will rarely accomplish anything positive and it can have long-lasting negative results.

19. *Maintain client confidentiality and trust.*

Confidentiality is an important ethical matter in most professions; it is even legally mandated in some. Interviewees should feel they can trust the interviewer to protect any information they reveal or any evaluation results obtained. In most professional settings, interviewers must obtain written permission to release any confidential information before it is provided to someone else. The exception, of course, is certain information that pertains to cases of neglect or abuse when the law dictates the reporting of such information.

In many settings, it is appropriate and helpful to discuss how confidential information will be treated. This allows interviewees to understand that what they say will be handled with dignity, respect, and integrity. This usually bolsters trust between the parties.

20. *Realize that change can be difficult and take time.*

The old phrase "Rome wasn't built in a day" applies to many interviewing situations, particularly those involving influencing, persuasive, or counseling types of interviews. There is a human tendency to resist change, particularly big changes. Many interviewees need time to process and consider new information or new ideas to begin accepting them before they can move toward adopting or implementing them. Interviewers may need to be patient and understand that many types of change take time. Sometimes, just considering some new idea is a major step for the other person; more complete acceptance and the actions deemed appropriate may come later. In some cases, we may have to push hard for change. In others, we run the risk of disrupting the process and eliminating the possibility of future change if we push too hard too quickly. Patience is needed in these types of cases.

21. *Make appropriate referrals when necessary.*

When interviewers encounter situations they do not have the training and experience to handle, or there is another person or agency that can handle some problem better, a referral may be necessary (Shertzer & Stone, 1980). Such a referral may be for legal or accounting counsel, medical consultation, psychological or psychiatric evaluation, or for services from a professional in one's own field who has more specialized experience or resources available.

Professionals, particularly those in educational, health, and human service fields, need to be comfortable with making referrals to others when it is in the best interests of the other party. The following suggestions are helpful to consider when making referrals.

- Be personally acquainted with professionals or agencies you refer to. Be familiar with services available in your community.
- Discuss the reasons for referral with the interviewee.
- Describe the types of information and areas of concern that the interviewee should share with the professional or agency to whom the person is being referred.
- Make sure the interviewee understands what information, if any, will be released to the professional or agency the individual is being referred to and how this information will be shared. (Adapted from MacLean & Gould, 1988; Sweeney, 1971)

With some linguistically and culturally diverse clients, especially those with a language barrier, more help may be needed to facilitate a referral because multiple agencies and procedures can be confusing.

Some interviewees are hesitant to act on certain referrals, particularly those involving certain medical or mental health evaluations or those that can be costly. Terms like testing, evaluation, therapy, counseling, or other similar descriptors can be met with resistance. It is often better to use terms like "talk with" or "let's see what is found out from" rather than using more intimidating types of terminology. An interviewee's own statements and terminology can be used as a springboard for a recommendation (Lavorato & McFarlane, 1988). For example, an interviewee may say, "I've been so upset about _____ and I just don't know where to turn." The interviewer could use that as an opportunity to say, "I've noticed how much _____ is bothering you. Have you considered talking with someone who could you help with this? I'd like to suggest that you _____." This type of approach can be effective, because some of the client's own words are used, focus of attention is captured, and the person is helped toward a specific action.

22. *Deal constructively with failures.*

It can be difficult to admit, but there are some individuals we may be unable to help. There are many possible reasons for this—some people may not want our help, others may not be ready for it, some interviewees may not be willing to form a working relationship with us, and the list could go on. Interviewers must be honest with themselves about such possibilities and deal with them constructively.

All professionals have certain limitations and all make some mistakes. Admitting one's own limitations and inabilities to handle every situation perfectly are signs of wisdom and maturity. Kennedy and Charles (1990) have commented that professionals who cannot accept their own limitations and occasional defeats are in the wrong line of work. The growth of successful interviewers is related to discovering what works well, recognizing things that do not work, and trying constantly to discover "why." Growth is also predicated on learning and striving to improve, even in the presence of mistakes and failures (see Kottler & Blau, 1989).

23. *Evaluate your own effectiveness as a basis for self-improvement.*

To render effective services, professionals should regularly evaluate their own effectiveness. Such evaluations should be specific and objective. The interviewer can engage in self-evaluation by having a peer or a supervisor sit in on one or more sessions, using observational ratings or checklists (e.g., Amidon, 1965; Erickson, 1950; Hackney & Cormier, 1994; Ivey, 1994; McDonald & Haney, 1988; Molyneaux & Lane, 1982; Shipley, 1992; or others), reviewing audio- or videotapes of sessions, and by thinking objectively and critically. Spending a few moments after each interviewing session evaluating its effectiveness, its strengths and weaknesses, and areas that might be done differently next time, as well as more formal self-evaluations periodically, serve to identify counterproductive patterns that may have developed and thereby become a basis for self-improvement. These types of self-evaluations can help improve effectiveness and even increase levels of confidence.

24. *Learn more about interviewing as it pertains to your field and needs.*

This book has addressed a number of basic interviewing principles applicable across a number of fields and professions. There are many other resources available in bookstores and libraries that deal with interviewing; two of these we particularly like are Stewart and Cash's (1994) *Interviewing: Principles and Practices* and Garrett's (1982) *Interviewing: Its Principles and Methods*. Both are considered classics within the area of interviewing and both contain information that can be applied across many disciplines and occupations.

Many readers will need to develop skills, abilities, and further knowledge specific to their own profession. Additional information is available in bookstores, libraries, and trade or professional journals; at conventions, workshops, or seminars; or through supervisors and colleagues within the field. Availing ourselves of such opportunities can further bolster specific skills and abilities and increase overall effectiveness—which is precisely what most interviewers want for themselves and those they serve.

References

Amidon, E. (1965). A technique for analyzing counselor-counselee interaction. In J. F. Adams (Ed.), *Counseling & guidance, a summary view* (pp. 50–56). New York: Macmillan.

Anderson, P. P., & Fenichel, E. S. (1989). *Serving culturally diverse families of infants and toddlers with disabilties.* Washington, DC: National Center for Clinical Infant Programs.

Barbara, D. A. (1958). *The art of listening.* Springfield, IL: Charles C. Thomas.

Benjamin, A. (1981). *The helping interview* (3rd ed). Boston: Houghton Mifflin.

Black, J. M. (1982). *How to get results from interviewing: A practical guide for operating management.* Malabar, FL: Robert E. Krieger.

Brammer, L. M. (1993). *The helping relationship: Process and skills* (5th ed.). Boston: Allyn & Bacon.

Burgoon, J. K. (1994). Nonverbal signals. In M. L. Knapp & G. R. Miller (Eds.), *Handbook of interpersonal communication* (2nd. ed.) (pp. 229–285). Thousand Oaks, CA: Sage.

Casciani, J. M. (1978). Influence of models' race and sex on interviewees' self-disclosure. *Journal of Counseling Psychology, 215,* 435–440.

Clarke, P. A. (1968). *Child–adolescent psychology.* Columbus, OH: Merrill.

Cormier, L. S., & Hackney, H. (1987). *The professional counselor: A process guide to helping.* Englewood Cliffs, NJ: Prentice-Hall.

DeBlassie, R. R. (1976). *Counseling with Mexican American youth: Preconceptions and processes.* Austin, TX: Learning Concepts.

Dillard, J. M., & Reilly, R. R. (1988). The professional: An introspection of self. In J. M. Dillard & R. R. Reilly (Eds.), *Systematic interviewing: Communication skills for professional effectiveness (pp. 14–35). Columbus, OH: Merrill.

Dittman, A. T. (1987). The role of body movement in communication. In A. W. Siegman & S. Feldstein (Eds.), *Nonverbal behavior and communication* (2nd ed.) (pp. 37–64). Hillsdale, NJ: Lawrence Erlbaum Associates.

Donaghy, W. C. (1990). *The interview: Skills and applications.* Salem, WI: Sheffield.

Doster, J. (1972). Effects of instructions, modeling, and role rehearsal on interviewer verbal behavior. *Journal of Consulting Clinical Psychology, 39,* 202–209.

Drapela, V. J. (1983). *The counselor as consultant and supervisor.* Springfield, IL: Charles C. Thomas.

Edinburg, G. M., Zinberg, N. E., & Kelman, W. (1975). *Clinical interviewing and counseling: Principles and techniques.* New York: Appleton-Century-Crofts.

Edinger, J., & Patterson, M. (1983). Nonverbal involvement and social control. *Psychological Bulletin, 93,* 30–56.

Emerick, L. L., & Haynes, W. O. (1986). *Diagnosis and evaluation in speech pathology* (3rd ed.). Englewood Cliffs, NJ: Prentice-Hall.

Enelow, A. J., & Swisher, S. N. (1986). *Interviewing and patient care* (3rd ed.). New York: Oxford University Press.

Erickson, C. E. (1950). *The counseling interview.* New York: Prentice-Hall.

Fenlason, A. F. (1962). *Essentials in interviewing.* New York: Harper & Row.

Fretz, B. (1966). Postural movement in a counseling dyad. *Journal of Counseling Psychology, 13,* 335–343.

Garrett, A. (1982). *Interviewing: Its principles and methods* (3rd ed.). New York: Family Service Association of America.

Gelso, C. J., & Karl, N. J. (1974). Perceptions of "counselors" and other help givers: What's in a label? *Journal of Counseling and Psychology, 21,* 243–247.

Gilliland, H. (1992). *Teaching the Native American* (2nd ed.). Dubuque, IA: Kendall-Hunt.

Hackney, H., & Cormier, L. S. (1994). *Counseling strategies and interventions* (4th ed.). Boston: Allyn & Bacon.

Hall, E. (1964). Silent assumptions in social communication. *Disorders of Communication, 42,* 41–55.

Hartbauer, R. E. (1978). The first session—with whom. In R. E. Hartbauer (Ed.), *Counseling in communicative disorders* (pp. 3–21). Springfield, IL: Charles C. Thomas.

Haynes, W. O., Pindzola, R. H., & Emerick, L. L. (1992). *Diagnosis and evaluation in speech pathology* (4th ed.). Englewood Cliffs, NJ: Prentice-Hall.

Hutchinson, B. B. (1979). Dialogues: Client-clinician communication. In B. B. Hutchinson, M. L. Hanson, & M. J. Mecham (Eds.), *Diagnostic handbook of speech pathology* (pp. 1–29). Baltimore: Williams & Wilkins.

Insko, C., & Cialdini, R. B. (1969). A test of three interpretations of attitudinal verbal reinforcement. *Journal of Personal and Social Psychology, 12,* 333–341.

Irujo, S. (1988). An introduction to intercultural differences and similarities in nonverbal communication. In J. S. Wurzel (Ed.), *Toward multiculturalism* (pp. 142–150). Yarmouth, ME: Intercultural Press.

Ivey, A. E. (1983). *Intentional interviewing and counseling: Facilitating client development.* Monterey, CA: Brooks/Cole.

Ivey, A. E. (1994). *Intentional interviewing and counseling: Facilitating client development in a multicultural society* (3rd ed.). Pacific Grove, CA: Brooks/Cole.

Johns, G. (1975). Effects of informational order and frequency of applicant evaluation upon linear information processing competence of interviewers. *Journal of Applied Psychology, 60,* 427–433.

Johnson, R. (1988). Interviewing adults. In J. M. Dillard & R. R. Reilly (Eds.), *Systematic interviewing: Communication skills for professional effectiveness* (pp. 140–159). Columbus, OH: Merrill.

Kanfer, F., & McBrearty, J. (1962). Minimal social reinforcement and interview context. *Journal of Clinical Psychology, 18,* 210–215.

Kanfer, F., Phillips, J., Matarazzo, J., & Saslow, G. (1960). Experimental modification of interviewer content in standardized interviews. *Journal of Consulting Psychology, 24,* 528–536.

Keane, T. M., & Verman, S. H. (1985). The behavioral interview: Searching for clues to effective behavior change. In A. Tolor (Ed.), *Effective interviewing* (pp. 21–49). Springfield, IL: Charles C. Thomas.

Keefe, S. E. (1988). *Appalachian mental health.* Lexington, KY: University Press of Kentucky.

Kennedy, E. (1977). *On becoming a counselor: A basic guide for non–professional counselors.* New York: Seabury Press.

Kennedy, E., & Charles, S. C. (1990). *On becoming a counselor: A basic guide for nonprofessional counselors* (rev. ed.). New York: Continuum Press.

Kleinke, C. L. (1986). *Meeting and understanding people.* New York: W. H. Freeman.

Kottler, J. A., & Blau, D. S. (1989). *The imperfect therapist.* San Francisco: Jossey-Bass.

Kroth, R. L. (1985). *Communicating with parents of exceptional children* (2nd ed.). Denver: Love.

Krumboltz, J. D., & Thorensen, C. E. (1969). The effect of behavioral counseling in group and individual settings on information-seeking behavior. *Journal of Counseling Psychology, 11,* 324–333.

Lang, G., van der Molen, H., Trower, P., & Look, R. (1990). *Personal conversations: Roles and skills for counselors.* New York: Routledge.

Langdon, H. W. (1992). *Hispanic children and adults with communication disorders: Assessment and intervention.* Gaithersburg, MD: Aspen Publishers.

Lavorato, A. S., & McFarlane, S. C. (1988). Counseling clients with voice disorders. *Seminars in speech and language, 9,* 237–255.

MacLean, D., & Gould, S. (1988). *The helping process: An introduction.* New York: Croom Helm.

Marin, G., & Marin, B. (1991). Hispanics: Who are they? In G. Marin & B. Marin (Eds.), *Research with Hispanic populations* (pp. 1–17). Newbury Park, CA: Sage.

Martin, J., & Hiebert, B. A. (1985). *Instructional counseling: A method for counselors.* Pittsburgh: University of Pittsburgh Press.

McCroskey, J. C., Richmond, V. P., & Stewart, R. A. (1986). *One on one: The foundations of interpersonal communication.* Englewood Cliffs, NJ: Prentice-Hall.

McDonald, P. A., & Haney, M. (1988). *Counseling the older adult: A training manual in clinical gerontology* (2nd ed.). Lexington, MA: Lexington Books.

Mehrabian, A. (1968). Inference of attitudes from posture, orientation, and distance of a communicator. *Journal of Consulting and Clinical Psychology, 32,* 296–308.

Mehrabian, A. (1972). *Nonverbal communication.* Chicago: Aldine Atherton.

Meier, S. T. (1989). *The elements of counseling.* Pacific Grove, CA: Brooks/Cole.

Meier, S. T., & Davis, S. R. (1993). *The elements of counseling* (2nd ed.). Pacific Grove, CA: Brooks/Cole.

Merbaum, M., & Osarchuck, M. (1975). Modification and generalization of verbal behavior as a function of direct verbal intervention. *Psychological Reports, 36,* 775–778.

Molyneaux, D., & Lane, V. W. (1982). *Effective interviewing: Techniques and analysis.* Boston: Allyn & Bacon.

Moursund, J. (1985). *The process of counseling and therapy.* Englewood Cliffs, NJ: Prentice-Hall.

Moursund, J. (1993). *The process of counseling and therapy* (3rd ed.). Englewood Cliffs, NJ: Prentice-Hall.

Mowrer, D. E. (1988). *Methods of modifying speech behaviors: Learning theory in speech pathology* (2nd ed.). Prospect Heights, IL: Waveland Press.

Nellum-Davis, P. (1993). Clinical practice issues. In D. Battle (Ed.), *Communication disorders in multicultural populations* (pp. 306–316). Boston: Andover Medical Publications.

Nirenberg, J. S. (1968). *Getting through to people.* Englewood Cliffs, NJ: Prentice-Hall.

Okun, B. F. (1987). *Effective helping: Interviewing and counseling techniques* (3rd ed.). Monterey, CA: Brooks/Cole.

Okun, B. F. (1992). *Effective helping: Interviewing and counseling techniques* (4th ed.). Pacific Grove, CA: Brooks/Cole.

Orr, D. W., & Adams, N. O. (1987). *Life cycle counseling: Guidelines for helping people.* Springfield, IL: Charles C. Thomas.

Peterson, H. A., & Marquardt, T. P. (1994). *Appraisal and diagnosis of speech and language disorders* (3rd ed.). Englewood Cliffs, NJ: Prentice-Hall.

Phillips, J., Matarazzo, R., Matarazzo, J., Saslow, G., & Kanfer, F. (1961). Relationships between descriptive content and interaction behavior in interviews. *Journal of Consulting Psychology, 25,* 260–266.

Powell, W., Jr. (1968). Differential effectiveness of interviewer interventions in an experimental interview. *Journal of Consulting and Clinical Psychology, 32,* 210–215.

Purkey, W. W., & Schmidt, J. J. (1987). *The inviting relationship: An expanded perspective for professional counseling.* Englewood Cliffs, NJ: Prentice-Hall.

Rae, L. (1988). *The skills of interviewing: A guide for managers and trainers.* New York: Nichols.

Rich, J. (1968). *Interviewing children and adolescents.* New York: Macmillan.

Richardson, S., Dohrenwend, B., & Klein, D. (1965). *Interviewing: Its form and functions.* New York: Basic Books.

Riley, F. T. (1972). The effects of seating arrangement in the dyadic interaction interview upon the perceptual evaluation of the counseling relationship among secondary students. *Dissertation Abstracts International, 33*(4-A), 1447–1448.

Roberts, S. D., & Bouchard, K. R. (1989). Establishing rapport in rehabilitative audiology. *Journal of Aural Rehabilitative Audiology, 22,* 67–73.

Roseberry-McKibbin, C. (1995). *Multicultural students with special language needs: Practical strategies for assessment and intervention.* Oceanside, CA: Academic Communication Associates.

Rosenfeld, H. (1967). Nonverbal reciprocation of approval: An experimental analysis. *Journal of Experimental and Social Psychology, 3,* 102–111.

Samovar, L. A., & Hellweg, S. A. (1982). *Interviewing: A communicative approach.* Dubuque, IA: Gorsuch Scarisbrick.

Scheflen, A. (1964). The significance of posture in communication systems. *Psychiatry, 27,* 316–331.

Schulman, E. D. (1991). *Intervention in human services: A guide to skills and knowledge* (4th ed.). New York: Merrill.

Schum, R. L. (1986). *Counseling in speech and hearing practice.* Rockville, MD: National Student Speech-Language-Hearing Association.

Schuyler, V., & Rushmer, N. (1987). *Parent–infant habilitation: A comprehensive approach to working with hearing–impaired infants and toddlers and their families.* Portland, OR: IHR (Infant Hearing Resource) Publications.

Sharifzadeh, V. S. (1992). Families with Middle Eastern roots. In E. W. Lynch & M. J. Hanson (Eds.), *Developing cross-cultural competence: A guide for working with young children and their families* (pp. 83–104). Baltimore: Paul H. Brookes.

Shertzer, J. B., & Stone, S. C. (1980). *Fundamentals of counseling* (3rd ed.). Boston: Houghton Mifflin.

Shipley, K. G. (1992). *Interviewing and counseling in communicative disorders: Principles and procedures.* New York: Merrill.

Siegman, A. W., & Feldstein, S. (Eds.). (1987). *Nonverbal behavior and communication* (2nd ed.). Hillsdale, NJ: Lawrence Erlbaum Associates.

Smith, A. (1973). *Transracial communication.* Englewood Cliffs, NJ: Prentice-Hall.

Stewart, C. J., & Cash, W. B. (1994). *Interviewing: Principles and practices* (7th ed.). Dubuque, IA: William C. Brown.

Strunk, W., Jr., & White, E. B. (1979). *The elements of style* (3rd ed.). New York: Macmillan.

Sue, D. W. (1988). *Counseling the culturally different: Theory and practice* (2nd ed.). New York: Wiley.

Sweeney, T. J. (1971). *Rural poor students and guidance.* Boston: Houghton Mifflin.

Terrell, S. L., & Terrell, F. (1993). African-American cultures. In D. Battle (Ed.), *Communication disorders in multicultural populations* (pp. 3–37). Stoneham, MA: Andover Medical Publishers.

Thompson, J. (1973). *Beyond words.* New York: Citation Press.

Author Index

Subject Index